Daily Life in Indian Culture

An Insightful Guide to Customs & Traditions of India

(REVISED)

Thota Ramesh

www.ThotaRamesh.com

Other Books by the Author
(Available at www.amazon.com)

"Teamwork & Indian Culture"
A Practical Guide for Working with Indians

"Being Happy is Easy"
Go Beyond Positive Psychology,
Apply a Simple Technique for Eternal Happiness

DEDICATION

To Every Indian-at-Heart

CONTENTS

Preface

Welcome to India! - The land of different cultures. It is very fascinating to watch the great diversity in India. You get amazed by the various customs & traditions, the different religions/sects follow. But the interesting fact is that in spite of so many differences, there is a commonality in the way Indians live. The outward differences are mainly in the way the rituals are followed, but the underlying theme is almost the same.

If you are new to India, it would be very confusing and also stressful to interact with Indians. Even mundane things such as greeting each other, dressing up, sharing food, touching each other, etc. appear very complex and unnerving.

After reading this book, you will get a clear insight into the way Indians live and behave. You will be in a position to appreciate the rituals, customs, traditions of India. If you decide to spend some time in India or live with Indians, you should be able to get along with Indian way-of-life easily.

My goal is to communicate to non-Indians and *Indian Millennials,* the various facets of Indian culture in daily life; and the reasons behind those practices. Here, I am not referring to history; I am referring to the day-to-day rituals & traditions.

To build the story around these ideas, I have borrowed the characters from my earlier book titled **"Teamwork & Indian Culture – A Practical Guide for Working with Indians"**. In that book, I have mainly addressed the issues that directly affect the workplace behavior of Indians. On the other hand, this book analyzes all other Indian cultural aspects that affect the day-to-day life of Indians.

So, let us get going.

John - the hero of the earlier book "Teamwork & Indian Culture – A Practical Guide for Working with Indians" - has returned to America after spending six months in India.

The story continues from that.

---***---

1. Namaste

(Superstitions, Greetings, Physical Touch)

"Ahh-chchooooooooo!............" - A powerful sneezing sound reverberated in the hall. John tried to cover his mouth & nose in time with his hands to stop the droplets shoot-out towards the audience. He murmured 'Excuse me' and grabbed a couple of tissue papers to wipe his hands and face. He did notice a few 'Bless you' wishes that came from the audience and said "Thank you."

John is on the podium to share his experiences of India visit and to update the audience about the project. He caught a cold due to the travel and change of weather. He is excited at the opportunity to share his India experiences. Thanks to Dheeraj, his mentor at India office, he gained lots of insights into the Indian Culture.

"Thank you!" said John once again and continued. "As you all know the project has been completed successfully; thanks to the Indian team and all those here who helped me in this project. I am indebted to Mike for giving me this opportunity," said John turning towards Mike.

"Mike, I cursed you when you put forward this India visit proposal. But now I am grateful to you for pushing me on this. Apart from learning about managing a project, I learned a lot about India and about life. The credit goes to you. By the way, I gather that the audience here wants to know about my experiences in India too, along with the project updates. If you permit I will start with Indian experiences," said John and looked at Mike for approval.

Mike looked around, studied the mood of the audience and nodded affirmatively.

"Thanks, Mike,' said John enthusiastically. Since his return, John has been involved in many animated discussions about India & its culture. As this trip to India was his first trip abroad, the memories are etched strongly in his mind. He has been looking for opportunities to share and engage in discussions about India.

"As per Indian tradition, I should not start my speech now," said John with a gesture of helplessness.

"WHAT!" reacted some in the audience.

"Yes, I should wait for some time. Didn't you notice that I let out a big sneeze?" asked John and continued. "Sneeze in public functions is considered bad omen. Indians stop the activities and wait for few minutes for the person to recover. In India, they discourage people from sneezing in public functions. If someone has to sneeze, they have to move away from the public and sneeze discreetly."

"Come on! This sneezing is an accident and a natural phenomenon," remarked a member. "What is the big deal about it? It is superstitious to think that way."

"Yeah! It appears superstitious. But it has scientific reasons behind it. By the way, I discovered that many of the so-called superstitious beliefs do have meaningful reasons. Many of these reasons may not be valid now; as the time and circumstances change these traditions/beliefs lose their significance. It is for the society to be prudent about which traditions to continue and which to discard," said John and remembered Dheeraj. He felt as if Dheeraj is dictating those words to him, and he is cool about it.

"I am sure you all remember President Obama teaching a reporter in one of his press briefings, how to sneeze. After the outbreak of Swine-flu, we were all told to sneeze into our elbows/sleeves. Why?" asked John and paused for the reaction.

"It is for avoiding spreading of Swine-flu," responded a voice.

"Correct. If we sneeze into our hands, the germs will spread from one person to the other when we shake hands. Sneezing into our elbows is a good technique. But the sneeze shoots out particles very forcefully and the germs can land on people around. If you look at it, avoiding sneezing or moving away from the public to sneeze is a much better option." John waited for the audience to comprehend.

"So, that is exactly what the Indian tradition is promoting. They want people not to sneeze at public places as it can spread diseases easily. The Indian elders have rightly chosen a path of calling it a bad omen. Instead of explaining the scientific reasons behind this, calling it a bad omen is an effective way of implementing the desired behavior."

"One other interesting behavior I noticed about sneezing," said John. "Some of you have reacted to my sneeze with 'Bless you'. Interestingly, Indians do the same. They say 'Chiranjeeva'. It means 'live forever'. Even though our countries are at two ends of the world, the cultures have adopted similar behavior. I have a feeling that many of the traditions in different cultures might appear VERY DIFFERENT but the underlying phenomenon, the human aspirations seem to be the same."

"Very interesting!" commented Mike. "It can be a good subject for anthropologists and psychologists to study. Please continue," coaxed Mike.

John's face lit-up. The six months stay in India has completely transformed him. He feels that what he had learned in India in the last six months, is completely different than what he could have learned in his whole of life in the USA. It has been an incredible experience for him.

"Thanks, Mike," said John and continued. "On the same topic of Swine-flu, apart from the advice about sneezing, the health department has asked people to avoid shaking hands as the formal greeting. It is to contain the spreading of the virus. In this context too the Indian's way of greeting makes a very good sense. I guess you know what I am referring to..." asked John.

"Is it '*Namaste*'?" shouted one of the members from the audience.

"Yes. You are right. It is the formal greeting style of India," said John and folded his hands and gestured Namaste to everyone. "This way the people won't touch each other. Compared to western countries, the general public hygiene is poor in developing countries such as India. So this gesture serves the purpose of greeting and at the same time avoiding spreading of germs."

"By the way, this 'Namaste' gesture is accompanied by bowing. The literal meaning of Namaste is 'I bow to you'." John demonstrated the gesture again, this time along with bowing his head. "With globalization, this gesture is being replaced with a hand-shake. You see this happen in Urban India more."

"I heard the womenfolk don't shake hands with men. Is that correct?" asked a participant.
"Yes, and No," replied John. "By tradition, the girls won't touch boys and boys won't touch girls. Touching is allowed only in well-defined relationships. The trend is changing now, and girls are not hesitating to shake hands with men. And the Indian society is quietly accepting the change."

"One of the interesting ways of greeting is that of touching the feet. In almost all parts of India, the younger people in a family touch their elders' feet as a greeting gesture and take their blessings. This greeting i.e. Namaste and touching feet, is repeated while taking leave also. In some cases, they prostrate – it is called *Sashtanga Namaskar*. But it is usually done as a form of obeisance in religious functions and sometimes to appease a political leader."

"Appease a political leader?" said few voices.

"Yes, even though India is the largest democracy in the world, many of the political parties are run by a single powerful person, and by his or her heirs. So it becomes very important for the political leaders to demonstrate openly their loyalty to their supreme commander. So this prostration is one of them," explained John and waited for the reaction.

John looked at the audience and decided to stop talking about India. It has become very difficult for him to switch out of his monologue about India. Frequently he is getting carried away with the memories of India.

"I think I would stop here," said John and looked at Mike for approval.

"Thanks, John! You seem to have gained lots of knowledge and I see a great transformation in you," complemented Mike. "I personally would like to know more about India. We will have more discussions later. For now, please give a brief update about the project."

John switched on the projector system and started his presentation. He explained the challenges he faced while executing the project and how Dheeraj helped him out. Mike noticed the excitement in John's voice whenever he referred to the Indian cultural aspects of the challenges at work. Mike started wondering about the effect a visit to a foreign country can have on a person. His thoughts got interrupted with loud applause as John ended his presentation.

Mike thanked John and the team. While leaving the presentation room, Mike suggested to John that they should go out for lunch the next day.

---***---

2. The Marriage

(Arranged Marriage, Marriage Rituals, Caste, Joint Family, PDA, Indian Dress)

Ashley, the long-time live-in partner of John, is totally confused about John. After his return from India, she found him to be a completely different person. He appears to be more relaxed, but excited about every small thing in a positive way. She wondered what the real cause for this transformation is. Now, she is enjoying more not only her conversations with him but also his presence. He has become more accepting and open. Earlier he was very particular about everything, starting from brand of coffee to the way the house is set up. Many a time they had heated arguments about minor things, only to realize later how silly they were. Ashley noticed that those incidents have become rare and even in those cases it is she who was responsible.

Ashley has spent many hours listening to John's experiences in India. She is enjoying the way he narrates them. She feels he has developed a knack for storytelling, and she is now equally excited about India. She knows his Indian teammates - Dheeraj, Nasreen, Mallesh, and a few others so well as if she has met them personally.

One of the things Ashley is excited as well as confused about is 'the marriage'. She had discussed with John many times about getting married, but they could not come to a conclusion. John used to insist on continuing as live-in partners and was not ready to make a commitment. But after his return from India, there is a change. He seems to have made up his mind and had agreed readily for their marriage. Her thoughts got interrupted by the sound of the calling bell. It is John at the door.

"Hi Honey!" said Ashley and hugged John.

"Hello, Sweetie!" reciprocated John.

Ashley waited for John to freshen up and change into his night dress. John picked up a juice can from the fridge and snuggled next to Ashley on the couch.

"Do you know, John? I was just thinking about our marriage," said Ashley as a prelude.

"Go ahead Ashley!" encouraged John.

"To tell you frankly, I was taken aback when you have agreed for the marriage," said Ashley and continued. "You used to be non-committal. But I am glad you have agreed."

"I used to be..." stressed John and put his arm over her shoulder and pulled her close. "You are my love, and we have been postponing this decision for years," said John in a reflective mood.

"Not we. It is you!" pointed out Ashley.

"You're right," agreed John. "I am now a changed person. I used to think I should know more about you. Even though we have been living together for years, I thought I need more time to know whether we are compatible or not," confessed John.

"So what has changed now?" asked Ashley freeing herself from his arm.

"Nothing in the outer world, just my thinking and my perception," replied John. "My India visit has opened my mind to newer perceptions. There, almost all the married people I met have committed themselves to lifetime partnership. And the interesting point is that many of them got married after one and only one meeting."

"What! Getting married to a person after a single meeting?" exclaimed Ashley jumping in her seat and facing John.

"Yes!" replied John. "It was a shocker for me. For example, Dheeraj met his wife of 20 years in her house along with a few other family members. He, as well as the girl, had to decide in that meeting itself, whether they want to get married or not."

"Unbelievable!" said Ashley with her mouth wide open.

"That is the fact. That is the tradition. It is changing now. The family elders used to choose the boy or girl based on the family background as well as the person's background. The elders check the compatibility of the families. That is the first thing. By the way, they prefer to marry within their community i.e. caste."

"What is this caste?" asked Ashley.

"I will tell you more about it later. But consider it as a sub-community within the larger community of Hindus. There are marriage bureaus and online portals for choosing people from within one's own community. Interestingly, I have seen the marriage bureau advertisements for sub-community within Christians also."

"You mean there is caste system in Christianity also!" said Ashley with a puzzled look.

"Yes, the people who got converted from Hindus carry their identity of caste also," said John.

"Coming back to Dheeraj, he wanted to talk to his fiancée before marriage. But his fiancée's father did not give permission. So he had to assert himself to take the girl out for one hour. And you know what?" waited John, for dramatic effect and said,

"His fiancée met him along with her younger brother."

Ashley could not stop laughing. She tried to imagine the plight of Dheeraj. She felt it to be hilarious.

"Poor Dheeraj!" said Ashley and asked curiously. "What did he do then?"

"It seems he asked the boy to sit at a table far away from them. And then he had a private conversation with his fiancée," explained John.

"Very strange," commented Ashley. "How can they marry without really knowing each other? How can they develop intimacy?" said Ashley thinking aloud.

"It is amazing," commented John. "I attended a marriage of one of Dheeraj's nephews. They have elaborated rituals to perform during the marriage. Dheeraj has explained them in detail to me. Many of the rituals are aimed at developing the intimacy between the bride and bridegroom."

"Did I tell you that girls and boys who are not related are not allowed to touch each other?"

"Yes, you mentioned it one time. But you also said that the culture is changing now and they now shake hands as a formal greeting," reminded Ashley.

"Yes! Yes!" said John. "The marriage rituals were developed very long time ago. Apart from many rituals aimed at appeasing God, there are many aimed at developing a bond between the bride and bridegroom. Let me elaborate," said John sitting straight up. Now, both of them are facing each other on the sofa and resting their backs onto couch's hand-rests.

"You can appreciate the rituals if you assume that these two persons have not touched each other so far. So keep that in mind and follow me," instructed John.

"One of the acts involves pressing one's toes by other's feet, called *'Pada Mardanam'*. Another act is to put a paste made of edible items on each other's head. Later both are asked to hold their hands together – called *'Pani Grahanam'*. And they are asked to go around the sacred fire seven times reciting seven vows of marriage holding their hands."

Noticing that Ashley is listening intently, John continued, "To encourage intimacy they included few games also. They might appear childish, but that is exactly what they want to promote i.e. make them play with each other as kids. One of the games is to pick up the gold ring thrown into water contained in a vessel with a small mouth. It gives them an opportunity to be physically close and experience the touch. In another game, they are asked to pour the rice grains coated with turmeric powder – called '*Talambralu*' - over each other in a playful competitive manner. In some traditions, they ask the bridegroom and bride to play throw & catch flower ball," explained John.

"Interesting!" said Ashley. "Even in our tradition, we have games as part of pre-marriage ceremonies."

"Yes, but they are more of Adult nature," commented John. "This is the major difference between western and eastern cultures. The Indians do not show affection of Adult nature in public. What I mean is kissing and hugging as lovers in public is not encouraged. It is to be kept private."

"Why? You say that Indians celebrate life. What is wrong with the public display?"

"Great question, Ash!" said John and continued. "You can compare it with TV and Movie ratings. Every program in our country is given a rating – G, PG, PG-13, R, NC-17- to cater to Children, Teens, Adults, and Mature Adults. Everything happening in the public we should consider it as a TV show that is for the youngest of the audience. Do you show an Adult movie to a child?" asked John.

Noticing that Ashley is thinking about it, John continued. "The beauty with Indian culture is that they give equal importance to other relationships between opposite sexes – mother, sister, daughter, aunt, sister-in-law, niece, friend, student, mentee, etc. And the interesting thing is that you have different roles to play and you get lots of happiness, joy from the love and affection from all these different roles."

"So, the husband & wife, or lovers relationship is one of the many relationships. And I guess Indians do not want that to dominate other relationships," said Ashley thoughtfully.

"Absolutely! And I liked that concept," said John. "If we both love each other a lot, and we know that, what is the need for us to showcase it to the public? It is personal. We should be happy that we know we love each other," declared John.

"I agree," said Ashley. "It appears Indian marriage customs are fun, I think we should get married in Indian style," said Ashley jestingly.

"That will be great," said John. "On a serious note, we should try to live together as husband and wife till we die."

"Come on John! We sure will," assured Ashley by getting up and hugging John.

"This commitment is one of the seven vows of Hindu marriage," said John as Ashley moved away from him.

"But John," said Ashley hesitatingly and looked into John's eyes. He nodded his head to say go ahead.

"Do you think...." paused Ashley and said, "Are Dheeraj and his wife happy?" Initially, she wanted to ask whether they would be happy as she is yet to make up her mind about John's transformation.

"That is a million Dollar question!" said John with excitement and sat on the couch straight. He felt good about the way the conversation is happening. It is a long time they had a serious discussion about marriage and life.

"I too asked the same question to Dheeraj," revealed John and continued. "What he told me was very interesting and profound. By the way, he is visiting the USA next week."

"First," continued John, "Without blinking he told me that he was happy. And I could see that in him. He is always cheerful and appears to have no problems. He says he learned to be happy."

"Learned?" asked Ashley with a surprise.

"Yes. He practiced. Even though he is not a religious man he believes all religious texts are aimed at helping people to live happily. He specifically refers to Hindu scripture '***Bhagavad Gita***', the literal meaning is 'Song of the God'. He says this is a 'Practical Guide to Living Happily'. . The great sages of India compiled the wisdom into this form long ago. He said this book gives us very practical advice on handling life's challenges."

"OK," said Ashley restlessly. "My specific question is about marriage."

"Sorry," said John as he realized that he got carried away with his thoughts on happiness.

"About marital problems, he openly agreed that they had many problems. And he said they were having, and also said they will be having."

"What!!!" exclaimed Ashley and pulled over the cushion on to her lap and leaned forward.

"Yes. His argument is that every relationship will have problems and especially close relationships. It is for the people involved to handle them as mature adults and grow from it. On his part, Dheeraj told me he promised his wife that he would never ever ask for a divorce. He says it is their culture. Whatever be the problems, they have to face them and solve them."

"Unbelievable!" said Ashley with her eyes wide open. "Here, we contemplate a lot about compatibility and try living together to check that out. There, two unknown individuals meet for a couple of times and decide to live together for life. Mind-blowing!"

"Is it only with Dheeraj? Or is it a common practice to get married this way?"

"Surprisingly, it is the practice in India. The trend is changing now, and the divorce rate is increasing. I asked Dheeraj 'what the secret is for Indian marriages to survive so long'."

"What did he say?"

"The fundamental reason he says is the joint family concept. In a joint family, many families live together. So in a home, you can find four generations of people living together. With those many people and different generations, everyone learns to adjust and everyone learns to accommodate."

"How many people live in Dheeraj's home now?" asked Ashley.

"For practical reasons, Dheeraj does not live that way physically. But psychologically he is a part of a big joint family of 50+ people. His brothers and sisters live separately, but they are together psychologically, emotionally. Any major decision in a family is still discussed in the whole family. Most importantly, any problem in the family is addressed by all. They meet very often and enjoy together. I personally experienced their love and affection on my visit to Dheeraj's village."

"Then, why is there an increase in divorce cases in India?" asked Ashley to bring back the focus.

"Dheeraj attributes the increase in divorce cases to break-down of joint family culture. In nuclear families, people are losing the ability to share, accommodate others' interests. It is expected that newlywed couples will have differences and that they need support. In a joint family, you have at least two generations of people to counsel and advice. Now with the break-down of that system, the newlyweds are left on their own to find ways to resolve. With women also having economic independence, both parties do not want to compromise. So, more and more newlyweds are seeing marriage counselors."

"It makes sense," said Ashley to herself. She is thinking about herself. How she wanted to be independent. How she moved out of her parents home to live an independent life.

John noticed the mood change in Ashley. He decided to cheer her up.

"Enough of this discussion, Ashley," said John. "You haven't tried wearing the '*Saree*' I brought from India. Right?" said John and got up from the couch. Ashley also joined him to the closet.

John picked up the two items he brought from India – one for her and one for himself. It is '*Saree*' – the seven yards cloth item – for her; and the '*Lungi*' – the two yards cloth item – for him.

They tried wearing them on their shorts by watching YouTube videos. John managed easily. But Ashley had to take John's help to wear the 'Saree'. After a lot of struggle and fun, she managed it.

Ashley looked gorgeous in the 'Saree'. Looking at her John said, "You look very pretty, Sweetie! Let me help you become a typical Indian woman."

He picked up a red lipstick from her make-up kit and some flowers from the flower vase. He made Ashley sit in front of him. He put a red dot with the lipstick on her forehead – the typical 'bindi'. Then he managed to stick a few flowers in her hair. He folded his 'Lungi' up and then walked her up, as she was tumbling over with the 'Saree', to the dressing mirror.

"Wow!" shouted Ashley with excitement.

"Compared to you, I look great in this Indian dress," said Ashley teasingly while adjusting the flowers in her hair.

"I agree. There is no doubt of it," said John holding her. "You know what, the Indians love life. And they accentuate the differences in male and female. So, women deck them up well with Bangles, Jewelry to appear distinct and beautiful. Just like you."

"Oh! Ok, Thanks. But...." said Ashley walking carefully back to the couch and settling down. "But this dress does not appear to be practical for work. Do women wear this '*Saree*' to work?"

"Yes, they do wear this to work! For your information '*Saree*' is worn by great political leaders as well as corporate heads such as CEOs and COOs," said John.

"What? CEOs and COOs! I can understand political leaders in '***Sarees***' as they have to represent masses. But in the corporate world too?" said Ashley with disbelief.

"Yes. The Chairperson of India's largest bank 'State Bank of India', the ISRO scientists who sent India's Mars Orbiter into space in 2015, Directors on many corporate firms – all wear '*Sarees*'."

"Let me show you some of the pictures I have taken in India," said John and picked up his laptop.

Both huddled together on the couch as John started showing the pictures of India. As they were seeing a photo of John's women colleagues in '*Sarees*' taken on a festival day, Ashley commented,

"I think John, the '*Saree*' fits well for every body type. It looks good on every one of them."

John agreed and they both got immersed in looking at the photos and discussing them. John pointed out the photo of Dheeraj and said,
"Ashley, he is going to be here in the USA. And Mike had asked him to give a talk on India."

"Oh! I see. Is it for your staff only?"

"Yes, it is for a small gathering. By the way, tomorrow I will be going out for lunch with my colleagues," said John.

Before they got up for dinner, they decided to visit John's parents to personally share their decision to get married.

---***----

3. Together or Separate

(Gender Behavior, Physical Touch, Happiness, Godmen, Food, Sharing, Superstitions, Languages, Indian States)

On Mike's suggestion, the team decided to go out for lunch to celebrate John's return from India. They went to a nearby restaurant and tried to find a quiet place, but in vain. The place is full of noise as people are reacting excitedly to the live telecast of NBA match on huge screens. The waitress seated them in a corner far away from the TVs. Mike thanked her and everyone settled. It was Mike's idea that they spend lunchtime together so that they can learn more about India from John.

As John took his place he could not avoid comparing this situation to the ones he has seen in India. A smile showed up on John's face as the images of Indian team lunches came into his mind. The women team members seating separately in a group; the men jostling friendly and physically patting each other. Mike noticed the smile and asked, "John, what is going on? You seemed to be amused at something!"

"Yeah! I just remembered the luncheon meetings in India. It is so different," answered John. "There the women team members almost always seated in a group separately from men. Even at parties they often stay together in a group separately from men," said John.

Looking at Ashok – a colleague from Indian origin working at USA – Mike asked, "Is it true Asok?"

"Yes, that is very much true Mike. In Schools and colleges, we boys used to hang-out separately from girls. We used to talk to girls keeping a safe distance from them. And in those days, we were not allowed to shake hands with girls. Now it is changing," explained Ashok.

"By the way, Ashok, I just noticed Mike calling you 'a-soak' instead of 'a-show-k'," said John and continued. "Dheeraj has given me a big explanation about the importance of pronouncing names correctly. But I have never seen you objecting to it."

"Hmmm…, I have given up correcting them John," replied Ashok. "They chose Dilbert's character's name for me. There it is spelled A-s-o-k, but my name is actually A-s-h-o-k."

The conversation got interrupted as the waitress was ready to take the orders. She took orders from everyone, collected the menu cards and left the place.

"The other thing that comes to my mind," said John and sat straight in his seat, "...is that the boys jostle each other, pat and hug each other more often. Almost everywhere I have seen boys holding each other's' hands and putting their hands over each other's' shoulders. In brief, having more physical contact than what we do here in our culture."

"Interesting observation, John!" exclaimed Mike. "Recently I have come to know about the levels of physical contact in different cultures, in an online course I have taken. This course has an interesting title **'Science of Happiness'**. It is an 'edx' course by Positive Psychology department of the University of Berkeley. In that, they mentioned that people in poor countries and developing countries touch each other more often than people in rich countries. And the interesting point is that the people in those countries are happier because they touch each other more often. It seems a positive way of touching increases happiness for all involved."

"Wow!" exclaimed one of the team members.

"That could be the reason we have professional cuddlers as we miss the natural touch experiences," continued Mike. "In New York, the cuddlers are charging as much as $80 per hour of cuddling."

"Maybe that is one of the reasons for a God-Woman to become famous in India," commented Ashok. "She is known as 'Amma - the hugging saint'."

"As John pointed out," continued Ashok. "We Indians of the same gender touch each other, hug each other, walk around holding hands or keeping hands on shoulders of each other more than what Americans expect," paused Ashok. "An interesting thing happened once. One day, I and few of my friends were enjoying ourselves in the swimming pool of our apartment complex. We were just having fun in our own way and suddenly a local boy asked me 'Are you guys, gays?' We did not notice that the kids were observing us with curiosity. Personally, I have nothing against gays, but I had to clarify to them that we are straight."

"By the way, John, what about women in India?" asked the only lady in the group.

"Oh! They express closeness much more," said John. "More than in the workplace, the women have physical contact a lot in parties, in social settings; and it is expressed more in rural areas. I have attended an Indian marriage and been to the ancestral village of Dheeraj. I noticed the women folk cuddling, hugging, joking and laughing a lot among them. It is so much fun to watch them happy and lost in their own world."

"Interesting! Looks like you are very fascinated by the women in India," said the lady. "Did you fall in love with anyone there?" asked teasingly.

"Come on! Ashley will kill me," said John referring to his live-in partner Ashley; and pushed his chair back as the waitress started placing the food on the table.

Looking at the food being served, the lady asked another question, "Ok I'll leave that topic there. But give me an honest answer at least to this question. Did you get the food you wanted, in India?"

"Oh, yes! In Hyderabad, there is no dearth of food varieties. You get every variety that you want. You have all big chains KFC, McDonald, Pizza Hut, Papa John's, etc. But I preferred the Hyderabadi food. It is spicy, but you can get it done less spicy and it tastes so good. The greatest thing that I found out is that there are umpteen numbers of varieties in Indian food itself. Contrary to general belief many of them are not spicy," explained John as he picked up food with his fork.

"And each state has its own variety," continued John, "and within a state itself, the cuisine is different from one locality to other. For example, in Hyderabad you find *Rayalaseema*, *Andhra* and *Telangana* cuisine which belong to the Telugu speaking people."

"Who are these Telugu speaking people?" asked the lady.

"Oh, let me explain," said Mike, eager to share his knowledge of India.

"India is a diverse country. People speak different languages at different geographical locations. So the Indians divided their country into various states based on the most popular language spoken in that region. The city of Hyderabad is in Andhra Pradesh where the people speak a particular language called Telugu," said Mike with an air of authority and pride.

"But.....," said John & Ashok at the same time. John looked at Ashok and nodded his head to say go-ahead.

"But, a small correction," said Ashok. "Recently the Andhra Pradesh state has been divided into two states – Andhra Pradesh and Telangana. Basically, the Telangana state has been carved out of Andhra Pradesh. Now the Hyderabad city is in Telangana. With this new state, we have 29 states in India."

"And seven Union Territories," added Mike, not to lose the opportunity to showcase his authority on the subject.

"The other revelation is that you get a meal at as low a price as 25 cents. Many a time, the food served at streets is good and tasty as they make it fresh. India is amazing that way – it allows every economic section to survive. Not just with food, almost all services are available at hugely different rates. For example, a haircut can cost you $10 in a star hotel, but a common man can get a hair-cut for Rupees 10 i.e. for few cents," summed up John.

"Wow, it is really amazing!" exclaimed entire group.

"By the way, I have uploaded some of the photos that I have taken in India to the site www.ThoDu.org/Thora. You can see this 10 Rupees haircut photo there," said John.

One of the members in the party got onto the site on his mobile and started looking at the photos. Everyone else was busy finishing their food while wondering about India. The noise of cutlery was interrupted by the words "Is there anything else I can get you?"

Everyone looked at the waitress who asked that question and replied in negative.

"Oh! OK. Hope you enjoyed your food," said the waitress. And asked the most important question,

"Checks! Together or separate?"

"Separate," said Mike.

As the waitress left, John face was lit with excitement, and he sat straight in his chair. He leaned forward and said, "Let me share with you yet another interesting thing with Indians. In my entire stay in India, I was never allowed to pay for my food while eating out with them. Indians compete against each other to pay the whole bill. Many times, it becomes embarrassingly difficult for the waiter to choose which one to accept."

"Hey, I came across a very interesting book recently 'Together or Separate Checks? By Shaomin Li'," said Ashok. "I haven't read, but it appears to be a great book that explains the differences between Eastern and Western cultures. On first look it appeared to me that Indian & Chinese cultures have lots of similarities," concluded Ashok.

"Interesting!" said John. "I was puzzled by this behavior to compete with each other to pay the bill. So I reached out to my mentor Dheeraj for answers. As you know he has great insights into their culture. He told me that there is a wide disparity in incomes among friends and close relatives. That is the reason for this behavior."

"John! don't give teasers. Elaborate it," pulled up Mike with authority. Mike has lots of respect for Dheeraj. Whenever Dheeraj's name is mentioned, he becomes alert and would like to know more what Dheeraj says and thinks.

"Ok, let me explain," said John and cleared his throat. "In a school, for example, children from different economic status join and learn together. Some of them cannot even afford to have proper food or dresses or for that matter shoes. And some of them come to school in high-end cars; and are super rich. But all of them become friends as they are studying together. These differences are known to all of them and it won't come in the way of their friendship. Now, what happens is that whenever they go out together, whoever has the money he would pay."

"So the poor guys won't contribute anything, any time?" asked the lady.

"Contribute?" repeated John. "The poor guys also contribute. Not money, but through services. They will take the lead in providing any physical services that are required. But remember, it is all voluntary in a group. Nobody keeps a tab on who did what and how much a person has contributed etc. It is expected of everyone to do whatever they can contribute as loyal members of the group," explained John stressing the word 'contribute'.

"When they grow up also, many of them maintain the same friendship and relationships. I know in Dheeraj's family there are people who live in a single room and there are people who live in mansions. But when they meet for any social event, you will not be able to see any differences in their behavior. They enjoy together without any qualms."

"Awesome! A great way to live in a society," commented Mike.

"About food, there is another interesting thing I noticed while I was traveling in a Train," said John and waited to see if everyone is interested in listening.

"Whenever a person in the train wants to eat some snacks or food, they first offer it to co-passengers. Many times, they insist on others taking at least a token of food before they themselves can have it. I was told by Dheeraj it is customary in India to share food with others in the vicinity. And one should always offer food to the guests whatever be the time they visit."

"Yeah! That is true," said Ashok. "Our mother used to say if you do not offer and others ogle at your food; it will cause harm to you i.e. you will fall sick. It is called bad 'Dhrishti' - the evil eye. That is the main reason people share food with others."

Before John countered that view, the waitress started giving out the checks to each of them. John looked at his check and gave the money to the waitress. John waited for everyone to pay the waitress and motioned to them to sit down.

"Great fact Ashok," said John. "I studied many of these superstitious beliefs and rituals as I was curious about everything Indians were doing," continued John. "With the help of Dheeraj, I could understand them in the right perspective. Even though many of rituals and beliefs appear to be irrational and superstitious at the outset, they all have a strong reason, rationality behind them. It is true some of the reasons may not be valid in the current context & environment, but they were valid when these rituals were introduced."

John looked around and continued, "For example, take this case of bad 'Dhrishti' Ashok has referred to. The wise men in India decided that it is good for society to share food, especially when there is a vast disparity in the economic conditions of people. So to enforce that behavior, almost in all cases, the wise men resorted to creating fear among people i.e. one will face punishment by God or Devils if they do not obey the diktats."

"I agree with you John," said Mike approvingly.

"Even in our culture, you come across many superstitious beliefs. And I am sure there was some good reason at the time of introducing those customs," said Mike rising from his chair.

Everyone got the cue and rose from the chairs; and thanked John for sharing his experiences.

"Oh! I forgot to tell you guys. Dheeraj is landing here tonight and he agreed to give us a talk on Indian rituals at various life events. And he warned that it could be a long session", said Mike.

Everyone nodded in acknowledgment.

---***----

4. Life events

(Caste, Gods, Hindu Rituals, Life Cycle (birth-to-Death), Arranged Marriage, Divorce, Joint Family, Uniform-Civil-Code)

"Good evening!" said Dheeraj addressing the small gathering in the Lecture hall. Dheeraj is at the podium on John's request to explain Indian way-of-life to the team. John has projected Dheeraj as an expert on Indian culture. So everyone in his team wanted to listen to Dheeraj about India.

Dheeraj continued, "I am not sure what John has told you about me. Let me first confess I am not an expert on Indian Culture. Whatever I shared with him and going to share with you, is based on my personal experiences and observations. As you all know, by profession I am a Software Delivery Manager and Quality head. I have applied the same analytical skills and reasoning that we use in our profession, to understand the way things work in the world. So, please do pay attention and critically review whatever I say. Interrupt me. Question me. It will help clear my thoughts also."

"What do you say?" asked Dheeraj.

Everyone nodded their heads in affirmation and felt comfortable listening to Dheeraj.

"One important disclaimer before I start," said Dheeraj and paused. "I am a Hindu by birth. So, whatever I share with you today are traditions/rituals followed by Hindus in general. As you know India is a diverse country. You see diversity everywhere. No single place is uniform. There are many religions and thousands of Gods; many languages, many regions; and within a community many castes and sub-castes. It is impossible to generalize and share anything common across the whole of India. The only thing I can say is that Indians love life. And the colorful rituals, traditions are aimed at celebrating life."

"With this introduction, let me take you through the typical Hindu traditions in one's life," continued Dheeraj.

"In Hindu philosophy, every living thing is treated as God. And every creation whether it has life or not is believed to be the creation of God. Life is considered a gift from God. And every life form has to fulfill its duty on this earth. Many of the rituals, traditions were evolved to help the human being sail through life easily. These traditions, rituals are passed on from generations to generations; and now some of them may not be relevant, or do not serve the purpose it was originally intended for," said Dheeraj as an introduction.

"Let me take you through the life cycle of birth-to-death. Let us start the cycle from a mother-to-be. Similar to the baby shower, a religious ceremony is held invoking Gods to protect the mother and the baby. This is usually a women-only event. The expecting-mother is decked up well and there will be music and dance to celebrate the event. In some communities, the mother is given gifts. Unlike in Western countries, the gifts are not meant for baby rather they are meant for the expecting mother. Any guesses why?" asked Dheeraj.

There were murmurs, but no one came forward to answer.

"It is because of the uncertainty," said Dheeraj and paused for the effect. "...Uncertainty about baby's birth. Due to various reasons, the infant mortality rate was high. So, people pray to God for a successful delivery. Even after the delivery, until 21 days the baby is not given a name and the baby is not draped in new clothes – only cleaned old clothes are used. No new clothes or toys are bought. It is to avoid the unnecessary memorabilia in case the baby does not survive," explained Dheeraj.

"Now the infant mortality rate has come down, but the tradition continues. The 'Naming ceremony' of the baby becomes the major event. It is usually conducted in the 3rd month. At this time, the gifts are meant for the baby's use."

"Interesting," commented one from the audience. "Here we have to choose a name before the baby is born. And as we won't know the gender, we have to be ready with a suitable name – one for boy and one for the girl."

"Starting from the Naming ceremony, there are various events that are celebrated throughout the childhood," continued Dheeraj. "Some of them are *'Annaprasanam'*, *'Mundan Ceremony'*, *'Aksharabhyasam'* etc. *'Annaprasanam'* is an event for feeding solid food to the baby. *'Mundan Ceremony'* is about shaving the head of the baby and *'Aksharabhyasam'* is initiating the baby to learn alphabets. And there are many more rituals and ceremonies in between these and they are celebrated differently in different communities," said Dheeraj and paused for a while.

"But," continued Dheeraj, "The interesting fact is that almost all of these rituals are happened to be associated with a particular age of the child; For example, *'Annaprasanam'* is performed at the age around 6 to 8 months."

"Any guesses how these rituals across India happened to be in sync?" asked Dheeraj.

"Going by the way you are explaining, Dheeraj," responded a lady. "I think all these are timed with the baby's normal growth pattern. If I am able to follow your thought process, I guess these rituals help the new parents and their family to observe the baby's growth."

"Awesome! Great explanation," said Dheeraj. "Please give her a big hand," requested Dheeraj.

Dheeraj waited for the applause to end and then continued. "Unlike here in the USA, we do not have training sessions for parents-to-be or for new parents. We do not have a formal mechanism of passing on this knowledge. The knowledge and wisdom are passed on from generation to generation through customs, rituals, celebrations. Because of this, the elders have great importance in society. The new generations were dependent for their survival on elders. I said 'were dependent'. It is no more valid, as the information and knowledge are available at fingertips in this era. So the customs, rituals are losing their importance."

"We have rituals to celebrate the onset of puberty too," said Dheeraj and continued. "It is a way of announcing the major milestone in the life of a child to the general public. It helps the community to know about the presence of a matured adult in that family. In old times it is a way of announcing the eligibility of a child for the marriage."

"By the way, how many of you know that majority of marriages in India are arranged marriages?" asked Dheeraj. Dheeraj looked at the hands raised and noticed that the majority of them are aware of it.

"This is an intriguing thing for many. I was asked many times, 'How can you marry a person without actually knowing her or him?' That is the question the *Millennials* in India are also asking now. In our culture marriage is not just between two individuals, it is between two families. So the elders assess the family and the girl. Then they provide an opportunity for the boy to 'see' the girl" Dheeraj paused as he noticed that the audience got a little confused.

"Hope I have not confused you," said Dheeraj apologetically.

"The important fact to note is that the family plays a major role in deciding whom to marry. As we were brought up in this culture, both the boys and girls are mentally prepared for this arrangement. Even in this arrangement, we have a provision to back-out. This is provided in the form of the engagement ceremony. This ceremony is conducted a couple of months before the marriage. So, the boy and girl have a couple of months to know each other and decide whether to move forward or back-out," explained Dheeraj and assessed the mood of the audience.

"The current generation is different now. Now they are more inclined towards love marriages. The concept of boyfriend and girlfriend has caught up. It is not yet so serious that every boy should have a girlfriend or vice-versa."

Pointing to the audience, Dheeraj said, "If YOU do not have a girlfriend or boyfriend, you are still OK!"

Everyone laughed.

"Due to the global cultural influence and improvement in economic conditions, we are now witnessing many divorces in India. The stigma of breakup or divorce is no more a serious thing. People in India are becoming more and more independent. This in turn, is leading to nuclear families and the collapse of joint families. So, the social pressure/influence is replaced fully by the legality of actions. Now, Indians want to play by the book i.e. they want to ensure that their actions/relationships are valid in terms of the law of the land. So, the love-marriages, live-in relationships or gay relationships are catching up."

Dheeraj stopped and asked, "Hope I am not boring you. I just got carried away by the fact of the collapse of joint families."

"No! No! You are fine," said the audience in unison. "We are here to know more about your culture. Go ahead!"

"Thank you. As I see it the concept of joint families is the great strength of Indian Culture," said Dheeraj and took a sip of water.

"Let me explain the core idea behind the Indian cultural customs. The vibrant culture of India with lots of rituals, ceremonies have evolved to ensure a happy life. In the absence of systematized knowledge dispensation and the absence of a strong civil, criminal code implementation, Indians are guided by the social customs and norms. Many of the customs are in place to ensure public acceptance - mind you public acceptance, not legal acceptance. Even now there are many communities that overrule the Indian law and enforce their own customs. It is a very serious problem in rural India."

"Sorry to interrupt you, Dheeraj. Do you have a uniform civil code? I heard each religion has its own laws," asked Mike.

"You are right, Mike," said Dheeraj. "We do not have a uniform civil code yet. Within the constitution, they made provisions for each religion to retain their own laws subject to validation by the constitution. The courts continue to debate over these issues time and again. Recently the Supreme Court of India is debating about the '**Triple *Talaq***' rule of Muslims. As per the 'Triple *Talaq*' rule, a man can divorce his wife by saying '*Talaq*', '*Talaq*', '*Talaq*' i.e. by saying it three times. It seems some of the Muslim men are conveying that through Facebook as well as through WhatsApp to get a divorce. So, recently a 35-year-old Muslim woman - Shayara Banu - has approached the Supreme Court seeking a ban on 'Triple *Talaq*' and few other customs. It is a long way road for Uniform Civil code in India."

"Coming back to Hindu rituals, one last thing I want to share is about death. The rituals conducted at the time of death of a person are elaborate. When my father expired, I have followed and observed those rituals very closely. Leaving out the rituals that are meant for appeasing God, almost all of the rituals had some purpose. Just bear with me as I explain it to you," requested Dheeraj emotionally.

"First, the dead body is given a bath in front of the public. A few elders from society supervise the bath. The elders will take a close look at the body and see if there are any abnormalities/injuries. This is one way of ensuring that there is no foul play. Later the body is placed for the public to pay their respects. Again the public gets a chance to look at the dead body and if there is any doubt about the nature of death, it gets discussed and police will be informed."

"In Hindu customs, the body is cremated. The family will wait for all the close relatives to arrive before the cremation takes place. This ensures that everyone is informed about the death of the relative and allows them to be together to support the immediate family," explained Dheeraj and looked at the audience for their continued interest in this topic.

"There is an interesting ritual just before the cremation takes place. The dead body is placed on the ground next to the cremation area; and the children of that person are asked to shout into the ears of the dead person 'Papa/Mama' – whatever they are used to address the person. Can you guess why?" asked Dheeraj.

"A last-minute check, I guess," said a person from the audience. "Just to check if the person is still alive."

"Absolutely right!" said Dheeraj. "There are instances where people came out alive from the dead."

"After cremating the dead body, the children have to visit the cremation site after a couple of days and collect the ashes. If you look at it from the society perspective, it ensures that dead bodies are disposed of properly."

"And in Hindu customs, there are ceremonies for 11 days from the day of cremation. During these days all close relatives, extended family members gather in the house of the dead. And during these days it is mandatory that one family from the extended family should sponsor food etc., on one day of these 11 days. Again, it is a social contract to ensure that close relatives support the grieving family. During these 11 days the immediate family members of the deceased are not allowed to go for work; for that matter go out of the house. This again ensures that the kith & kin of the deceased gets a chance to fully grieve. It helps the family members to cope with the loss of a loved one and complete the grief cycle as they say in Psychology."

"Finally, if the family has marriageable daughter, as per the custom they should get her married off within one year of the death. On the other hand, if the marriage of son is fixed or about to take place, they should postpone it by one year i.e. they should perform the marriage only after a year."

"I think you understand, why?" said Dheeraj and continued. "A girl's marriage involves spending lots of money. So, whatever the savings the deceased person has accumulated should be spent right away for the marriage. In the case of a son, there is a fear that wife-to-be for the son - might influence the son to divert the finances away from the family."

"In conclusion, many of the rituals have some useful purpose or a reason. But they are not very easy to comprehend. Hope I did justice to the time you spent with me. Thanks and if you have any questions, I can address," said Dheeraj bowing his head and took his seat.

The hall reverberated with the applause. Mike thanked Dheeraj on behalf of the audience.

While leaving the hall Mike said, "Dheeraj, we should meet one day over a drink. I have been reading more about Indian culture, and your talk further increased my interest in it. I would like to get your opinion about some of the things I learned about India."

"Sure Mike, I am ready any day. Let me know your convenient day and time. You fix; and I will come," assured Dheeraj enthusiastically.

"Please don't forget to invite me," said John as he and Ashok joined them.

As Dheeraj noticed Ashok, he turned towards Mike and said, "By the way except this Friday. I promised Ashok that I will have dinner at his house."

"Dheeraj, Ashley & I want you to join us too for a dinner," said John.

"Sure John, but you told me that you are visiting your parents this weekend. I will definitely have dinner with you both on my next trip," assured Dheeraj.

---***----

5. Train Journey

(Indian Village, Train Journey, Emotional Goodbyes, Epics, Privacy Invasion, Sharing of Food, Toilets, Rickshaw)

Ashley is excited about the idea of meeting John's parents. She talked to them a couple of times and even had a Skype video-call once, but this is the first time they will be meeting. She looked at John. He appeared relaxed even after the five-hour drive from Chicago. They were in Chicago a day-before and decided to drive down to his parents' place. The Toyota Sienna they are in is cruising smoothly at 65 MPH. Ashley noticed that John is occasionally focusing his gaze on the road signage. They crossed Cincinnati a while ago. And John is looking out for the exit he needs to take for his parents' home town. This town is just half-way between Cincinnati, OH and Louisville, KY.

"Yeah! This is the exit!" said John, flipping the right indicator and slowing down to take the exit.

Ashley noticed the excitement in John. But she also noticed the sudden increase in her heartbeat. She is excited about meeting John's parents, but at the same time, she is very nervous. Her relationship with John goes back to a few years. They have been staying as live-in partners happily and wanted to continue that for years to come. With John's visit to India, things have changed.

After his return from India, John had a series of discussions with her and convinced that they should get married. This trip to John's parents is to break this news and get their blessings.

John skillfully took the exit and got onto the country road. John looked far into both sides of the road. The road is lined with huge open agriculture lands with automatic sprinklers moving on them; and farmhouses somewhere in the middle of those fields. There is no trace of people anywhere. Occasionally he saw buffaloes and few horses on those fields. Even though he grew up here everything is appearing differently to John. He is all eyes and is savoring every detail. On the contrary, Ashley was not paying any attention to the surroundings and she is lost in her thoughts. She turned towards John to say something and is surprised to see him getting immersed in the view outside.

"Hey, John! Are you visiting this place for the first time?" asked Ashley teasingly.

"No, no!" said John and sat up straight in his seat and patted Ashley. "All of a sudden all these things are appearing different to me," said John as a way of explanation. "The six months of stay in India has changed my perspective. It is compelling me to compare and take a relook at everything in my life, including these surroundings that I was brought up in. The images of Indian village are flashing in my mind. I had been to Dheeraj's ancestral home in a village. It is so different," said John and waited for Ashley's response.

"What is it like? Tell me all about it," requested Ashley coyly, hoping that this conversation would brush aside her thoughts about meeting his parents and the anxiety associated with it.

"All right," said John taking a deep breath. "Let me narrate it in such a way that you can visualize it. Relax and enjoy the rest of the one hour drive as if you were in an Indian village."

"It all started with my request to Dheeraj to see an Indian village," said John remembering the event.

"Dheeraj, I want to visit a village in India," said John all-of-a-sudden while they were having tea.

John met Dheeraj's enquiring gaze and to clarify Dheeraj's doubt, he repeated.

"Yes, I want to visit a village in India. Can you help me with it?"

"Sure John, I can. But why this sudden interest in an Indian village?" questioned Dheeraj.

"You see, I have been in Hyderabad all this time. I have seen and learned a lot about urban Indian life. While talking to the team members here, I realized almost all of them are from nearby towns and villages. They moved to Hyderabad and are staying in rented accommodations. What I noticed is that they were all excited to go back to their hometowns at every opportunity. Some of them told me that they spend every weekend in their villages, towns."

"That is true. Great observation John," appreciated Dheeraj. "Like a sponge, you are absorbing everything about India. Maybe you can start a business as Indian culture consultant after going back to the USA," commented Dheeraj.

"On a serious note, I am also from a village," continued Dheeraj. "For the sake of the job, we all moved to Hyderabad and settled here. My parents are no more, so no-one from my immediate family lives there in the village. Now, this has become my home town," said Dheeraj while gazing into infinity.

John noticed the feeling of resignation in Dheeraj's voice. "Looks like you are also longing to visit your village," said John sympathetically.

"Can we go there for a weekend?"

"Sure. Some of my cousins still live there. They will be happy to see us. But, be prepared. You will not have these 3-star facilities there," cautioned Dheeraj.

"No problem, Dheeraj. I am game for it. I love adventures and nature. I am used to camping. I am sure I can handle it," said John excitedly. "For that matter, I want to live a life of a true Indian just to sink in the feeling."

"Ok great. I know you have the determination and required adaptability. So, let me make arrangements for it. I will give you the real taste of India," assured Dheeraj.

The following Friday evening both John and Dheeraj were settling down in their seats in a 3-tier compartment of Visakha express at Secunderabad Railway station. Dheeraj has booked non-a/c 3-tier compartment berths to his village. It is going to be an overnight journey.

John is all excited. This is the first time he boarded a train in India; for that matter in his life. All this while, he has been traveling by air and road only. The only time he had a sort of train experience is at Disney World, where they transport people from parking lot to the main entrance.

While entering the Railway station, John felt as if he is entering a stadium. There were so many people coming out and going in. He had to push himself through the crowd to get on to the platform. It was very noisy with people talking, hawkers shouting, TVs blaring, and loudspeakers making train announcements. Dheeraj showed the big display system to John and they noted down the platform number for their train. Dheeraj motioned John towards the bridge to cross over to the desired platform.

As they were walking towards the bridge, John looked around. He found the station to be very clean even though there was so much of crowd. He noticed stalls along the walls – book stalls, snacks & beverages, toy shops, etc. He also noticed hawkers reaching out to the passengers in the train. He politely said 'no' to a railway porter who approached him offering his services. He was surprised to see escalators in this railway station. Both John and Dheeraj took the escalator and crossed the bridge to reach their platform. Dheeraj checked compartment number and identified their berth numbers. The 3-tier system allows 3 people to sit down on well-cushioned bench during the day. And by lifting the backrest, they can convert into a sleeping berth for Middle. With that, there will be 3 berths – Lower, Middle and Upper. After placing the luggage under the seats, Dheeraj got down the train. John occupied the window seat and was watching Dheeraj. Dheeraj bought a few magazines and two mineral water bottles and boarded the train.

As the train started moving, there was a rush of people getting down. John realized that they were the people who came to see the other passengers off. He noticed so much of commotion at that time; people waving hands and shouting to say good-bye & take care. It was fun. Some people were straining themselves to look at their family members on the platform through the grilled windows. And some people on the platform were running along with the train to steal a glance and to wave at their loved ones in the train. He noticed tears rolling down from some of them. He was surprised to see so much emotion and wondering what was going on. His thoughts got interrupted by Dheeraj's question.

"How are you feeling, John?"

"Oh! Great! I am enjoying every moment of it. First time I am seeing so many different emotions at the same time. I have been in crowded places such as sports stadiums, beaches, concert halls, prayer halls; there you see only a few common emotions. It is completely different here," said John with his eyes wide open.

"Yeah! Your observation is correct. Every person in this train will have his own story. There is so much diversity here that you can write a story about each person on this train. That could be one of the reasons that India ranks top in story-telling," said Dheeraj.

One of the co-passengers who was listening to them joined the conversation. "You are right sir," he said to Dheeraj and turned towards John. "Sir, in India we have two great epics written long, long time ago. They are '**Ramayana**' and '**Mahabharata**'. Both convey a lot about human values, emotions and the travails of life."

John was taken aback by this sudden intrusion. He noticed that everyone in their coupe is listening to them and that they are watching him curiously. He felt a little uncomfortable.

"Thanks, sir! for telling my friend about epics," said Dheeraj to assure the person that he is welcome to join conversation.

Suddenly that man shook hands of Dheeraj and John. And he enquired Dheeraj who he is and who John is. And he exchanged his contact information with Dheeraj. Few others also joined in this bonhomie. And the discussion turned out to be a group discussion. John could not understand everything as they switched into local language Telugu most of the time. During the discussion, one of the co-passengers opened a snack box and offered it to everyone around. John hesitated to take it but accepted it after Dheeraj's prodding. The same sharing of food happened during dinner time even though John & Dheeraj got theirs from the Railway catering services.

The time went by quickly. John is enjoying himself thoroughly and is surprised to see unknown people becoming so close within a matter of minutes. It was almost like a party among close friends. As it was past 9:00 PM, they decided to sleep and converted the backrest into a berth; and everyone occupied their respective berths. The discussions continued even while lying down on the berths till late into the night.

John felt a pat on his back. It is Dheeraj, waking him up as their destination is approaching.

"Wake up John. In the next 30 minutes, we will be reaching our destination. You can brush, and use the restroom before that," informed Dheeraj and reminded John to take toilet paper with him.

John got up and went to the restrooms area of the couch. He found both Indian and western style toilets. He opted for western style, brushed his teeth and used the loo. He has become an expert in using the health faucet – a fancy name for the faucet at loo - the Indian way. He washes himself with water from the faucet and wipes dry with the toilet paper. Dheeraj has advised John to carry toilet paper with him as it won't be provided at many places. Luckily for John, the toilet paper was available along with the faucet at all places in Hyderabad i.e. in the 3-star hotels as well as in the office.

John made his way back to his seat with a little difficulty as he had to wade through the people who were moving towards the exit doors. The train started slowing down. The co-passengers in their coupe shook hands with John and Dheeraj, and bid adieu. John and Dheeraj picked up their luggage and joined the others at the exit, waiting for the train to stop. Both got down from the train as soon as it stopped.

John looked around. It is a small station but very clean. As it is early morning, it is very quiet and pleasant. It appeared like a movie set to him. As soon as they were out of the Railway station a few people surrounded them. Dheeraj was politely shooing them away and started walking past them. John was wondering about the goings-on. Suddenly one person said Namaste to Dheeraj and gestured touching his feet and picked up the luggage from Dheeraj. Dheeraj patted that person and enquired about his well-being.

"John, this is Murali, lives in my village. He is a **Rickshaw** peddler. He will take us in his *Rickshaw* to our house," said Dheeraj. And then he introduced John to Murali. Murali said Namaste and took the luggage from John.

"John, hope you can sit comfortably in this *Rickshaw*. If you feel it is difficult, we can hire an auto-rickshaw," said Dheeraj and waited for John's reaction.

"No problem Dheeraj. I am ready to experience everything Indian. Let's go with Murali," said John and noticed the grateful expression on Murali's face.

The seating in this *Rickshaw* is different from that of others. The seats are not elevated. Both John and Dheeraj squeezed into it. Dheeraj sat down with legs crossed. But John is struggling.

"You want me to do Yoga on this Rickshaw?" mockingly asked John.

"Come on John. You can do it. This is just **Sukhasana**. Anyway! Stretch out your legs. But don't kick the poor fellow," said Dheeraj referring to Murali.

As they settled, Murali arranged the luggage in the rest of the place on the rickshaw and got onto his seat to pedal the rickshaw.

◆ ◆ ◆

"How is the story so far?" asked John looking at Ashley.

"It is good! I am eager to know what happened in the village," said Ashley.

"Yep, I will do my best to give you a visual FEAST," said John as the thought of Dheeraj reminded him about Dheeraj's dinner meet with Ashok and the Indian food.

---***---

6. Tiger Mom

(Transportation, Physical Touch, Hygiene, Toilets, Parenting, Disciplining Kids, Schooling, Family Support System, Extended Family)

Ashok got up from his couch on hearing the calling-bell and opened the door. It is Dheeraj.

"Hi Dheeraj! Please come," said Ashok and led Dheeraj in. Dheeraj took a deep breath as he walked in and enjoyed the smell of the spices.

"Looks like Divya is taking lots of trouble preparing the food," said Dheeraj referring to Ashok's wife Divya.

"No Dheeraj garu! Nothing special," replied Divya with folded hands in the gesture of Namaste.

"Namaste Dheeraj garu! How is everyone back home in India?" enquired Divya while Dheeraj was settling down on the couch. Dheeraj replied; and three of them exchanged pleasantries. To a question from Dheeraj, Ashok mentioned that his kids were away at a birthday party.

"I just left them at Chuck-E-Cheese's. As you know we become full-time chauffeurs in America," commented Ashok.

"That is true. Unlike in India, here the children are wholly dependent on parents for their transportation i.e. dropping & picking-up," said Dheeraj. "Now I am enjoying my freedom in India, not only from my kids, but from my wife also. She now spends her time the way she wants without depending on me."

"I know. The kids can hop on to any bus or take an Auto-rickshaw. Here it is such a constraint!" said Ashok.

"Added to this, in our residential area we cannot even walk to Cub Foods. There is no footpath and you cannot walk on the road easily," lamented Divya as she sat down for conversation.

"I think in that context, India is a much better place. You have many different ways of transportation and at a very affordable cost. Sitting here in America, the public transport there appears to be a great boon," said Dheeraj.

"I agree," said Divya. "By the way, how are your kids adjusting to the life in India?" asked Divya with curiosity.

Dheeraj had moved back to India a few years back after living in the USA for several years. He gets to answer this question frequently.

"They are fine. Initially, they were put off by the unhygienic conditions and the way they were hugged by everyone in the family," replied Dheeraj.

"They used to get annoyed when unknown people i.e. unknown to them but are our family elders, take the liberty of touching them on the head or on their back. It took some time for them to accept it as affection."

"I can visualize that," said Divya. "Here the personal space is given lot of importance. And people consciously maintain a distance. What about unhygienic conditions?" asked Divya.

"That is the first thing they noticed as the major difference in USA and India. As soon as we came out of the airport and entered the city, they could see the roads littered with garbage. And they saw people dumping the waste onto roads from buses and cars etc," explained Dheeraj. "They refuse to accept it as normal and carry a plastic bag with them to use it as a trash bag."

"The children here are very particular about it. That is one great habit the kids learn here," said Divya agreeing with Dheeraj's observations.

"On a long drive to my village, I had a tough time finding a toilet i.e. rest room for my son. As you know unlike here we do not have Rest Areas. And my son refused to relieve himself in the open."

Both Ashok and Divya giggled.

"He insisted on finding a toilet. My wife got irritated and said 'Why are you behaving like a girl? Why are you so shy?' But he won't budge and luckily, I found a decent restaurant on the way," explained Dheeraj.

"Yeah! It is a major issue in India," said Divya. "For that reason, when traveling with elderly people in India, I choose railways as they have toilets within every coach."

"More than my kids adjusting to India, I found it tough to adjust to my kids' point of view," said Dheeraj. "In this situation the way my son reacted is correct. As he has spent his formative years here he sees things differently."

"I know," jumped in Ashok. "My kids don't listen to me. They question everything. It is very stressful raising children here," poured-out Ashok with anguish.

"That is very true, Dheeraj garu. Ashok and kids have differences always and I have to play a mediator role. The kids have grown up and have independent views," said Divya.

"What grown up! They are not even teenagers," said Ashok. "I am worried about what will happen once they become teenagers. Now itself, they do not obey me and they are not scared of me."

"Ashok, we are brought up in a different culture. The rules are different now," counseled Dheeraj.

"Did you notice what you just said?" asked Dheeraj and paused for a while. "You want your kids to be scared of you."

Dheeraj looked at Ashok and Divya to see whether he should continue or stop.

"In our culture and in our times, we equated respect with fear. And our elders ensured that we are controlled by fear. Irrespective of our age, we are conditioned to respond with fear to our elders."

"I agree. My mother-in-law even now expects the same. If I don't get up from my chair when she is in the room, she gets offended. I respect her a lot but she won't understand," shared Divya throwing a glance at Ashok. Ashok squirmed in his seat uneasily.

"Many Indian parents are strict disciplinarians. It is because of the insecurity about the future which is natural as we are born in a developing country. Many of us use harsh measures to control our kids – publicly insulting, denying facilities; some parents go to the extent of punishing them physically too."

"That is Tiger Mom behavior," said Ashok. "A few years back a book by a Chinese mom created a sensation. It somewhat refers to what you are saying. This also highlights the similarities between Indian and Chinese cultures."

"I feel the economic conditions have a strong influence on the culture. The primary innate fear is that of survival. In an environment where there are fewer resources, we want our kids to out-beat others, compete fiercely and grab the available limited resources. We call that success," explained Dheeraj.

"Look at us," said Divya thoughtfully. "We left all our connections behind in India and came all the way to America for a better life. And this fear about children succeeding here is much more. It compounds more due to the entirely different culture they and we have to face. It is so stressful," said Divya with choking voice.

"It is all about adapting and making adjustments," said Dheeraj in a comforting tone.

"Sometimes, I feel the way some of us treat our children is like raising horses to win races. You breed the horses; give them the best food, the best training by carrot & stick method. From the horse perspective, it is just born for you to win the race," said Dheeraj and continued. "For example, I am not sure what to make of Thailand's '*Walk with Tigers*'. They tame wild animals for our pleasure. In the similar way, some of us feel children are our property and we want to prepare them to win the race that we have in our mind."

"That comparison is harsh, Dheeraj garu," objected Divya.

"It is just to highlight the point," clarified Dheeraj. "On the other hand, Western culture's way of raising children is seen as very passive. Our methods are construed to be abusing and Western's permissive. We interact with and treat our kids as Child, irrespective of their age. Our interactions tend to be from a dominant Parent to Child. Here, the Americans treat their small kids also as Adult. We need a balanced approach," elaborated Dheeraj taking ideas from the Transactional Analysis theory.

"Yeah, I saw the struggle of American parents in malls to control their little ones," said Divya. "They try to reason with kids."

"A slap on the bottom would have easily controlled the situation," said Ashok.

"That is the difference," said Dheeraj. "The Government here will consider that as child abuse. You might have heard about a TCS employee getting jailed in the Netherlands for sleeping on the same bed with their less than six-year-old kids."

"Yeah! I heard about it," said Ashok.

"Such is the difference in two cultures," said Dheeraj. "We as Indians are more violent at home compared to Westerners," said Dheeraj. "Earlier parents and teachers used to encourage harsh physical punishments. It is changing now. But the need for being competitive forces parents to instill fear in kids," concluded Dheeraj.

"I am confused," said Divya with a grim face. "What do I have to do as a Parent? How do I take care of my kids?"

"No single strategy will work," replied Dheeraj. "We need to be aware of the child's needs and change our approach. Based on the situation we have to provide required guidance. All our efforts should be to make the kid become a happy, independent and fearless person. Sometimes we have to hold their hand, sometimes we have to let go. As they grow, we should allow them to make informed decisions."

"It appears very complicated," said Divya thoughtfully. "Parenting is very demanding." Recovering from her mood she asked, "Dheeraj garu, our daughter will be getting into High-school next year. We are debating whether we should move back to India for her education. What is your experience?"

"As you know my son studied High-school here, and I feel he gained lots of important skills here," replied Dheeraj. "Personally, I feel the High-school study here prepares a person to live on his own in the world. They provide full exposure and experience of the real-life world. My son was taught BRS – Bank Reconciliation, in grade 6th. He learned how to write a check, how to balance the entries in Bank Passbook. He was aware of many of the things that are required for him to be on his own in the real world," elaborated Dheeraj and watched their faces for a reaction.

"Yeah! I agree. For example, they teach public speaking from early childhood," said Divya. "At Kindergarten level, they call it Show & Tell."

"Unfortunately, life skills are not given importance in the Indian Education system. It is focused on bookish knowledge. It needs a overhaul to meet the current environment's demands," said Dheeraj. "About my son, I can definitely say the High-school education here has made him more confident and independent."

"Apart from the education, her concern is about the culture here. Divya is worried about our teenage daughter growing up here," revealed Ashok.

"It is a genuine concern," said Dheeraj empathizing. "I guess the challenges of parenting a teenage kid are same irrespective of the culture. It becomes a burden here because you do not have the support system of extended family. Out there in India, the kids have uncles, aunts, grandparents, cousins to share their concerns and get counseling. So here you have to play all those roles. You have to be the friend, you have to be the non-judgmental counselor, you have to be the person with whom your kid can open up freely and share all their concerns."

"That is tough. We will keep in mind your inputs," said Divya and excused herself to attend to Kitchen work.

Dheeraj looked around. The two-bedroom townhome is neatly maintained. Divya had already arranged plates on the Dining table and he can hear the noise of curry being poured into serving bowls.

"Dheeraj, if you don't mind can I ask you a personal question?" said Ashok hesitatingly.

"No problem, what is it?" asked Dheeraj.

"About your Green Card," said Ashok. "You got Permanent Residence status, but why did you opt-out from it? Why did you go back to India?"

"Let me confess," said Dheeraj and cleared his throat. He had answered this question so many times. Everyone who knows about Green Card asked him the same question.

"To tell you frankly, I was not prepared to be a good husband and good parent all the time," said Dheeraj. Ashok could not believe what he is hearing.

Noticing the surprise on Ashok's face, Dheeraj continued, "In India, we get to play many, many roles in our extended family. Here I am confined to very few roles namely – Parent, Husband. It is the same case with my wife and children."

"Ok, what is it about GOOD husband, GOOD parent?" asked Ashok curiously.

"You see. In India, if we had any issues with our relationships, they get sorted out easily. There are so many well-wishers who can diffuse the situation and show the right way. Because of the nature of extended family, some of the family members' guidance is taken in the right spirit and followed. I used to miss that here."

"Let me give you a simple example," said Dheeraj. "In India you have visitors who knock on your door without prior appointment. It could be your relatives, friends or neighbors. Right?" asked Dheeraj.

Ashok nodded his head affirmatively.

"I am sharing a very personal thing with you now," said Dheeraj. "When I have a tiff with my wife it becomes very difficult to start a conversation with her. None of us will take the initiative, and wait for the other to do. The unannounced visit by a guest automatically forces us to interact with each other, thus breaking the cold war. Imagine that in America!"

"Yeah!" said Ashok. "I understand now. So to avoid tiffs you always have to be good. That means giving-in every time."

"That is just one thing. I would love to live in different parts of the world but would like to keep India as my home. I have been exposed to the love and affection of the extended family and the people around me. I think I crave for that and I like it. It is not a perfect world there. There are many things that need to be changed. If possible, I would like to contribute to it."

"What is it, Dheeraj garu? Are you planning to join politics?" asked Divya as she came to them to announce that dinner is ready.

Everyone laughed and moved towards the dinner table.

"We are missing John," said Divya. "Ashok invited him also as he loves Indian food, but he had other plans."

---***---

7. Village life

(Rickshaw, Village Scene, Hospitality, Extended Family, Eating Habits, Neighborhood Relationships, Caste, Reservation System, Education System, Government School, Toilets, Rituals, Queue system, Flowers in Hair-do)

"Let me take you back to the story," said John looking at Ashley.

"We boarded the *Rickshaw* and started our journey into the village".

As the *Rickshaw* moved slowly, John looked around. He became self-conscious as everyone's eyes are on him. People are gazing at him as it is the first time a foreigner appeared in that place. The *Rickshaw* got onto the main road and after a few minutes they were on a dusty road leading to Dheeraj's village.

The road is lined with huge trees providing a sort of canopy. Behind those trees were stretches of farmlands with green paddy. He saw some men walking into the fields. He noticed that some of them were having a mobile in one hand and a bottle of water on the other. Some people were just carrying a tumbler; it appeared to be filled with water.

Hearing a commotion John turned back to see. The street urchins playing on the road noticed the *Rickshaw* and started running after it. Murali was shouting at them to stay away from the *Rickshaw,* and started pedaling hard to get over the steep road. After a while, he got down the *Rickshaw* and started pushing it. When Dheeraj decided to get down to reduce the load, Murali objected. But all of a sudden, the *Rickshaw* started moving easily. The street urchins who were running along with the *Rickshaw* are pushing it from behind. Murali got onto his seat as soon as the steep road is over.

"John, did you notice how you have become a star, celebrity here?" asked Dheeraj.

"Yes, Dheeraj. Everyone is stopping their work and looking at me. I am feeling a little embarrassed."

"I think you are the first foreigner visiting this village. Be prepared to shake hands and, maybe, to give your autographs," said Dheeraj with a smile.

John did not respond as he was lost in enjoying the pleasant breeze. It is very refreshing; clean air and very less noise. He is very happy to be here away from the hustle and bustle of Hyderabad. At a distance, he saw women cleaning up their surroundings, sprinkling water and drawing some designs in front of their houses.

The dusty road ended, and the *Rickshaw* is moving on a cement road. This road is now lined with houses and shops on both sides.

"We have entered the village street," commented Dheeraj.

The people from those houses are looking at them straining their necks. Many of them waved at Dheeraj and greeted him with joy. Dheeraj responded to all of them and answered loudly to their questions. As they reached Dheeraj's cousin's house, the *Rickshaw* is surrounded by people of all ages. There was no need for Murali to stop the *Rickshaw*; it was already done by them.

Before Dheeraj could fully get down; people started hugging him, patting him and firing volley of questions at him. Dheeraj is completely immersed in being with them and is enjoying their love & affection. John left wondering about all that, and he stood next to the *Rickshaw* spellbound.

It took some time for Dheeraj to become free from the affectionate welcome. He is already inside the house and realized that John was missing. He went back to *Rickshaw*, introduced John to others and ushered him inside. One of the family members showed a room allotted for their stay and asked them to freshen up and join for breakfast.

John is overwhelmed with the reception. "Are all these people your family members?" inquired John.

"Yes John. Many of our family members live here in this village and in different houses. As they know that we are coming, all of them assembled here to receive us. I am meeting many of them, after a long time. So there is so much of emotion attached."

"Great to see that! In the midst of all that, I thought you have completely forgotten about me," teased John. Dheeraj gave a smile and asked John to get ready for breakfast.

Breakfast was arranged on a table. Everyone was waiting for Dheeraj and John. Dheeraj's uncle and his son joined them on the dining table. They have kept a fork & spoon for John's sake. Noticing that, John said, "I am fine eating with bare hands. I learned to experience the sense of touch apart from the smell, sight, and taste."

The hosts felt relaxed as John seemed to have adapted well to the Indian environment. They were a little worried about taking care of John. They talked to Dheeraj in advance about John's interests and preferences. As John is their guest, they wanted to ensure a great experience for him. They have prepared two varieties of each food item, one of them with less spice. But they noticed that John preferred the spicy food.

After finishing their breakfast, they moved to the veranda to meet people who were waiting for them. John is now getting used to seeing so many people. All of them were excited to see Dheeraj as well as John.

"Are all these people also your relatives?" asked John.

"No John! They are all my neighbors and known people of this village," clarified Dheeraj.

"But, I noticed them calling you Uncle or Brother. And you were also calling them with a relationship term!" said John with a confused expression.

"That is true John. Even though they are not my relatives, we call each other with a suitable relationship term based on age and gender. We are all like one family," explained Dheeraj.

"On the other side, I have seen some people addressing you 'sir' and the equivalent term in your local language."

"What? You could understand the local language also?" asked Dheeraj.

"Yeah! Their body language says it all," replied John proudly. "What is the explanation for their behavior?"

"Many of them are people who provide services to us. By the way, I should explain a unique feature in villages. As you might expect we have people to provide services of hair-cutting, washing of clothes, maid services. But people who provide a particular service usually belong to one particular community. Incidentally, this division of work has resulted in the Caste system, where each community got a particular Caste name. The other interesting fact is that in this village, like in many villages, each family from the service providing community gets to serve a certain number of houses in the village. That way all the members of the community get work," explained Dheeraj.

"Awesome arrangement," commented John.

"But it has led to one major problem - Casteism," said Dheeraj. "It is blind loyalty to one's own caste; and thus, leading to oppression and caste conflicts."

"Why oppression?" asked John.

"The communities that are well off wanted to protect their own interests. So, some communities were subjected to discrimination and were denied their rights. To undo this injustice, one of the first things the Indian Government has done after independence is to provide reservations to these discriminated communities in the areas of education and jobs."

"Oh! I see. Is this rule still in vogue?"

"Unfortunately, yes! even after 68 years of independence we still have this. This concept of caste-based reservations doesn't seem to have resolved the problem of inequality, but rather created strong divisive feelings among the people. And I feel it has further strengthened the concept of caste," said Dheeraj.

Noticing that some of the kids from the crowd were keenly observing them and hesitating to say something, Dheeraj stopped his discussion and encouraged the kids to open up. After hearing them he turned to John and said,

"John, as I told you, you have become an instant celebrity here. These kids want to take 'selfies' with you."

"Oh! No problem. I am honored. I won't get this type of attention too often," said John smilingly. The kids competed with each other and jostled to take the best selfie. John was now used to this physical proximity and pushing around, and sportingly enjoyed every moment of it.

Dheeraj went inside leaving John with the kids. He spent some private time with his Uncle and their family. After some time, he came out and enquired with John, "Is everything OK, John?"

"Absolutely fine," responded John. "I made new friends here and learned a couple of Telugu words. And we decided to play Cricket in the evening."

"Cricket?" said Dheeraj remembering the way he described the game to John long back comparing it with a baseball game.

"Hope you remember the rules that I explained to you," reminded Dheeraj. "By the way, if you are ready, I will show you around the village."

"Sure, I am ready. Let us go."

Sensing their plan, the people who gathered around John, left the place. Dheeraj informed his Uncle; and they stepped out.

"Everything in this village is in walking distance," started Dheeraj. "But when I was young, I used to feel these distances are very big; I refused to go by walk and used to demand for a bicycle. Now everything seems to have shrunk here. I think due to living in the city the perception of distance changes," reflected Dheeraj.

"Not just the perception of distances, many perceptions change due to new experiences," supported John. "I see in myself a great change after coming over to India. For me, the world is no more the same world that used to be."

"I noticed that," said Dheeraj and stopped at a gate with a huge compound wall. "This was my school, John. I studied in this school," said Dheeraj with excitement.

"Wow! Can we go in?" asked John.

"Sure. Today is a holiday. But I see a few people cleaning the school. Let us go inside," said Dheeraj and both went inside.

"This is a Government run school. I studied here till 10th grade. There were no fees. For that matter my entire education was sponsored by the Government as I come from the economically backward community," said Dheeraj.

Dheeraj introduced himself to one of the guys there. He, in turn, took them into Headmaster's room.

"This is the room of the Headmaster i.e. Principal," explained Dheeraj. "Look at that board John," pointed Dheeraj. It contained the names of 10th grade top rankers for each year.

"You will find my name there as I was the topper in my class."

"I see that," acknowledged John. The guy who allowed them inside was explaining lots of things to Dheeraj. John came out of the room and suddenly his eyes caught a familiar image. It is their company's logo.

"Hey Dheeraj!" shouted John. "How come our company's logo is here in this school?"

Dheeraj came out of the room and looked at the hoarding John pointed to.

"Let me explain. You see, those newly constructed rooms are toilets i.e. restrooms in your parlance. I have arranged for our company to build them for this school as part of the CSR program – Corporate Social Responsibility," elaborated Dheeraj.

"But, why toilets?" asked John with surprise. "Aren't they part of the school building itself?"

"Great Question," said Dheeraj in his typical style. "Arranging toilets is a huge problem in India. The schools and many buildings are constructed without proper toilets. And lots of homes in rural India do not have toilets. Many people in India use open spaces to defecate. This is a very well-known public issue but was never formally addressed. For a change our Prime Minister Mr. Narendra Modi has openly addressed this issue in his first Independence Day speech of 2014. He had announced a program titled '*Swachh Bharath – Swachh Vidyalaya*'. It means 'Clean India – Clean Schools'. As part of that program, the Government has asked private organizations to pitch in to construct toilets in schools."

"Oh! I see," said John, and peaked into the newly constructed toilet. It has an Indian style toilet and a bucket with a mug under a tap.

"You won't find the health-faucets here," said Dheeraj observing John's facial expression. "Western-style toilets, faucets might come up next. But I guess, the usage of toilet paper will remain an urban phenomenon for years to come."

"Ok. But I am unable to digest the idea that you construct buildings without toilets. The Government should not give permits to occupy the buildings that do not have toilets," declared John.

Dheeraj smiled knowing how the Government works. Many nasty images of not having proper toilets at Government buildings, colleges and homes came to his mind. He decided not to share that with John – a foreigner.

"I can understand how you feel about it," said Dheeraj empathetically. "Let me tell you about a ritual. To ensure a house is good for living, we have a custom called '*house-warming*' ceremony. As part of that custom, the lady of the house must boil milk in the kitchen of the new house. Can you guess why?" asked Dheeraj.

"For the obvious reason – for daily food," replied John. "To ensure that the kitchen is in working condition."

"Correct. I think we Indians should now include a new ritual. We should say, to flush out any bad omen from the house to be occupied, a ceremony should be held in the toilet and flushing should be done."

"Wow! Great idea," exclaimed John.

"By including a ritual and instilling a sort of fear could be a good way to ensure toilets are part of every building. This is how most of the rituals come into practice," concluded Dheeraj.

Their discussion got interrupted by the giggling of the guy at the school. He was amused by the discussion that John and Dheeraj were having.

Dheeraj took John around the school. It is a huge place with many classrooms along the border, with wide open space in the center for the play area. There are various courts marked for different games. Dheeraj went down his memory lane and shared some of his adventures & misadventures with John.

Dheeraj thanked the guy who accompanied them in the school and came on to the street. As they were walking past a shop next to the school, one old lady called out Dheeraj's name. Dheeraj turned back and greeted the old lady affectionately. The old lady had a chat with Dheeraj and offered some snacks that she is selling. Dheeraj took them and when he was about pay she refused to take the money. But Dheeraj forced her to take a note of Rupees 100 and in return, she gave him blessings.

"I used to buy snacks from her during school breaks. She still remembers me," said Dheeraj emotionally; and offered the snacks to John.

Both started munching on them and stopped by a Tea stall. The Tea stall is a small hut with few wooden benches in front of it. As they approached it, the people who were sitting on the benches stood up and did 'Namaste' to Dheeraj and moved aside. Dheeraj responded with a 'Namaste' and motioned them to sit down. But they refused to do so and a couple of them stopped sipping their tea also.

"Namaste! *Babai*," said Dheeraj to the guy who is making Tea. The owner of the tea stall recognized Dheeraj and came out of the hut.

"Namaste Dheeraj! How are you? It has been so long?" said the guy with great excitement and dusted the bench for them to sit.

John has heard Dheeraj addressing elderly men and women in different terms.

Babai – Father's younger brother
Mamaiah or *Mama* – Mother's brother
Atthaiah or *Attha* – Father's sister
Chinnamma or *Pinni* – Mother's younger sister

He uses these terms even though they are not his relatives. This is the custom to indicate that everyone is part of a big family. Unlike the English language, Indian languages have well-defined terms for addressing each of the relationships on both mother's side and father's side. And a slight twist to a particular relationship term such as *Mamaiah* and *Mama,* differentiates formal and informal relationship. In the morning, John's head went into twirls as Dheeraj was introducing his family members.

Dheeraj asked *'Babai'* about his family's wellbeing. The guy called out a girl around 20 years of age and introduced her to Dheeraj. The girl is his daughter studying Engineering with Computer Science, and he asked Dheeraj to provide career guidance to her. As Dheeraj was advising the girl, other boys and girls joined them. It had become an impromptu counseling session.

"Dheeraj, special tea for both of you," said *'Babai'* while handing over the teacups to Dheeraj and John. He stopped his work, stood there with folded hands while Dheeraj lectured the kids. At the end, he thanked Dheeraj profusely and took his phone number. Here again, when Dheeraj offered to pay, *'Babai'* refused to accept the money.

"Did you notice how poor this *Babai* is?" asked Dheeraj.

"I can imagine," replied John looking at the small shack and noticing the fact that his Engineering daughter is helping in chores at the tea stall.

"One very good thing that is happening in India is that people have realized how important education is. One educated person in a family can completely transform the family and bring them out of poverty. My father always insisted on us getting higher and higher degrees. Even though we are a big family and there was a need for additional income to feed the family, he did not force any of us to work. He refused to focus on amassing wealth. He always told us education is important for you to become a complete person and wealth is incidental," said Dheeraj in an emotional tone.

He cleared his throat and continued, "Luckily, many of the parents have realized the importance of education; and are making extreme sacrifices to ensure their children get educated. This tea stall *Babai* is an example."

"Very commendable," supported John. "And I noticed you get very emotional about education and do free counseling whenever there is an opportunity. I appreciate you," commented John respectfully.

Dheeraj took John around a few streets. During this tour, they stopped at a couple of houses of Dheeraj's relatives and friends. Everywhere they were received affectionately and were asked to have lunch with them. Dheeraj politely refused by saying his cousin has made preparations for the lunch already.

As they entered the cousin's house, John could smell the pleasant & pungent smell of spices. His mouth started watering. The same smell in his initial days in India used to give him repulsive feelings. It once again reinforced his learning of how perceptions & feelings change based on the experiences one has.

Dheeraj and John were served a sumptuous meal. The ladies of the house served the food personally. John was surprised to see Dheeraj being scolded and shouted at for not tasting all the items. What amused John most was the fact that Dheeraj enjoying being treated like a kid by his sisters-in-law and by his cousin. For a minute, John felt Dheeraj to be a completely different person. He never saw this part of Dheeraj's personality. But he liked every minute of it and realized that his eyes were getting moistened.

After the lunch, John went to the room allocated to them leaving Dheeraj behind. After a few hours Dheeraj joined John. They relaxed for a couple of hours and decided to go for an evening walk. This time, Dheeraj took him to outskirts of the village. They saw many women working in the huge green paddy fields. John could notice a Tractor in the middle of the field. He remembered reading somewhere that the farming in India is still labor-intensive - very less use of machinery. They saw a temple at a little distance. Dheeraj and John walked towards it. While on the way they have to wade through the cattle that are returning home from grazing. Both had to watch their steps as the road is littered with cattle excreta.

The entrance to the temple is lined up with eateries, and shops selling items required for performing prayers, toys for kids. Dheeraj pointed out an eatery and said, "John, do you see that crowded eatery place? It is the best eatery in our village. They make excellent *mirchi-bajjis* – a spicy snack of stuffed Chilli."

John looked at that direction. There is a guy frying things in a big deep-frying pan. And he is surrounded by 15 to 20 people. Everyone is falling over the other to give their orders to that guy. The guy has an assistant who is collecting the money from many people at a time and skillfully handing over the correct items to everyone. There are some shy people and kids who were struggling to get the attention of the assistant to place the orders. It appeared very chaotic, but everyone is being served.

"Dheeraj, I noticed this system in Hyderabad also. Why can't you guys have First Come First Serve system? See few guys are forced to wait as they could not push their way," pointed out John.

"I agree with you, John. This needs to change. As you have rightly said, here the mighty gets his way. Because of this, you don't see women coming forward to buy things in this type of place. Implementing the Queue system i.e. First Come First Serve, will go a long way in improving equal opportunities for everyone," mused Dheeraj.

While walking towards the temple, John noticed almost all of the ladies buying small jasmine flower garlands called '*gajras*' and decorating their hair-do with it. Very few ladies have used a single flower such as rose in their hair-do.

Noticing John's gaze, Dheeraj commented, "They act as natural perfumes apart from making the ladies look beautiful."

As they reached the entrance of the temple, Dheeraj pointed out the shoe corner to John. Both of them left their shoes with the lady manning that corner and entered the temple barefoot.

John understood very well why they have to leave the shoes outside. While coming to this temple, John had to walk carefully to avoid stepping on many dirty things, such as cow dung, on the road. John surprised to notice that many people were walking on the road without any footwear. At Dheeraj's cousin place, they offered him water to clean his feet. Here in this temple, they have provided taps to wash feet. They roamed around the temple appreciating the beauty and did not enter the temple as there is a big Queue for 'darshan' i.e. seeing the deity.

The sun had set, and it had become dark. John looked up and noticed a clear sky full of stars and the moon. Suddenly he realized that he does not remember the last time he watched the sky in Hyderabad. In that crowded city with tall buildings, and with a busy life there was no opportunity for stargazing. "What a pity!" he thought.

As they walked back home, John noticed small groups of people of all ages chatting while sitting outside their homes - on cots, on wooden benches, on the ground, on platforms made of stone & cement. They all seemed to be immersed in the moment and appeared to be very happy. Many of these houses are made of bricks and the rooftops are covered by tiles. Some of them are huts - made of mud and covered by palm leaves. Very few houses are having RCC roofs – Reinforced Cement Concrete – and Dheeraj's cousin's house is one of them. But almost all houses have open space around them.

Dheeraj & John were received by Dheeraj's cousin as they entered the house. He enquired with John if everything is OK for him. John replied affirmatively. Once again, they had sumptuous food. This time there were a few more people in the house. They were all here, not for Dheeraj, but to have a glance of John. The entire village is excited about a foreigner visiting their village.

While John and others were having dinner on the table, the rest of the people sat on the ground in 'Sukhasana' style and in a row. They were being served food on plates made of leaves stitched together.

John had noticed the same in some restaurants in Hyderabad also, i.e. food being served on leaves such as plantain leaves. As usual John got a very good explanation from Dheeraj. These are natural stuff, biodegradable and good for nature. They replace plastic and paper plates. On the same context he pointed out about use of handkerchiefs made of cloth instead of paper napkins/tissue papers. He agreed there is a trade-off between convenience and environmental considerations.

After dinner, they went to the terrace and were joined by a few elders; some of the kids also joined them. One of the kids pointed out about the Cricket game and John had to apologize for not keeping the promise. The kids asked John many questions about America and the life there. John answered all of them, but few times struggled to explain as he never thought about those issues deeply. Later some of them sang songs and asked John to sing one. It was very entertaining.

While this is happening, Dheeraj was talking to his cousin and finalizing the next day's program. Dheeraj's cousin announced that it is time for sleep. Everyone wished each other good-night and dispersed.

◆ ◆ ◆

"That is how our first day was in the village," said John.

"Very interesting! The visuals seem to have etched in your mind clearly," said Ashley. "What did you do the next day?"

"Dheeraj's cousin arranged a car for us to do sightseeing, and the same car dropped us back to the railway station also," explained John.

"Oh! I see."

"So, we went back to our room for sleeping. You should see what Dheeraj wore as a night dress!" said John.

"What was it?" asked Ashley.

"I will explain," said John.

---***---

8. Ritualization

(Indian Dress, Indian Ornaments, Make-up, Bindi, Toilets, Worshipping Plants, Weekly Market, Hindu Monk, Holy-cow, Spices, Rangoli)

John looked at that road and said to Ashley, "Another 20 minutes we should be there." He is referring to his parents' house.

"I think we are a bit late," said Ashley looking at her watch. "Your story of India is the culprit."

"Yeah! That is fine," said John and continued. "I was telling you about Dheeraj's night-dress, right? Let me continue."

"Hey, what is this you are wearing?" asked John pointing to the cloth Dheeraj has tied around his waist. John has seen people wearing that cloth on the streets and thought that to be a poor man's dress.

"This is called '*Lungi*'," answered Dheeraj. "Very convenient to wear, you just have to wrap it around. But you better be sure to tie it well to your waist, otherwise it can lead to a wardrobe malfunction," said Dheeraj in a cautionary tone.

"Most of us wear it as night-dress and casual dress at home. But it is also a formal dress in many southern states in India. You find it being used in many South Asian countries too," explained Dheeraj.

"So, women wrap '*Saree*' around themselves and men wrap themselves in '*Lungi*'. Right?" said John.

"You are right. Do not say 'wrap', John. Wearing a *Saree* is an art. The same seven yards cloth is worn in many different styles. You can guess the region a lady belongs to by the way she wears the *Saree*," explained Dheeraj.

"Wow! I didn't realize that."

"And there is '*Shawl*'' that we wear over our upper body – over the shoulders and sometimes over the head," continued Dheeraj. "By the way, men wrap their lower body in very long cloth too - called '*Dhoti*'. This is also tied at the waist. If you see the pictures of Gandhi – our father of Nation – you will find him in *Dhoti* and *Shawl*," elaborated Dheeraj.

John wondered if Indians were late to adopt sewing and stitching.

"Another thing Dheeraj, I have not seen a single girl wearing Jeans or pants here. And, I have not seen these beautiful dresses in the city," said John.

"Yeah! Wearing pants, Jeans is a western culture phenomenon. It is more prevalent in cities. It caught up in towns but not reached the villages yet. The dresses worn by these village girls are called '*Parikini-Voni*'. These are our traditional dresses. You will find even urbanites wearing them on traditional days," explained Dheeraj.

"Another thing I noticed, the girls and women are decked up well here. I saw many of them having the red-dot on their foreheads, necklaces on their necks, and bangles on their wrists. One difference in girls and women that I noticed is that many women were wearing toe rings and many girls wearing anklets."

"Wow! Watson! You have become a great observer," said Dheeraj in Sherlock Holmes style.

"All these are to accentuate the differences between men and women. The red-dot on the forehead you referred to is called '*Bindi*'. It is a Hindu custom. Even men put on *Bindi*, in a little different style, as a mark of religious custom. The toe ring indicates that the woman is married. Apart from that ornament, Hindu married women wear a special necklace called '*Mangalasutra*'."

"Oh! Ok. As you always say about traditions, Dheeraj, do these traditions also have some scientific reasons?" asked John.

"They do have reasons. They are social in nature," said Dheeraj. "Many traditions are introduced with the intention of social order and not necessarily for the health aspects. For example, I feel the reason for making girls wear noise making bangles and anklets could be for ensuring their safety. But there are many over-patriotic and pseudo-scientists who keep on attributing skewed logic and scientific explanations in terms of health or otherwise to these. That is unfortunate. I heard some living intellectuals giving a scientific explanation for wearing silver toe rings, and about everything Indian. Be skeptical and arrive at your own conclusions."

Looking at his watch Dheeraj said,
"Good night, for now, John. We need to wake up early."

"Good night," said John.

The next day John woke up early and went into the attached bathroom to get ready. As he was coming out of the bathroom, Dheeraj woke up and asked, "Is everything OK, John?"

"Yeah!" said John and continued. "I just had to struggle a bit using the Indian style toilet," said shyly.

"Oh! OK. Consider as if you have gone out to camping in the wilderness," empathized Dheeraj and reminded John about his love for adventures. Their discussion got interrupted as the maid brought tea along with the message that a car is waiting for them.

After having tea they collected their luggage and stepped out of the room and into a hall. John saw six boys sleeping in one corner of the hall and in the other corner a few girls. It reminded John of his sleepover days.

As they came out of the hall to the open courtyard, John noticed a lady doing prayers, going around a plant placed on a pedestal. She has tied a towel to her wet hair, has red powder as a big '*Bindi*' on her forehead and has yellow color paste applied to her feet. She appeared to have just taken a bath and started this prayer. She is pouring water little by little to the plant and praying to it with reverence.

He noticed the entire courtyard to be clean and wet with a sprinkling of water mixed with something that he could not recognize. The ground is decorated with beautiful drawings.

Dheeraj bid farewell to his cousin and other family members. John joined him in that. One of the women members handed over a packet containing food items for their breakfast. Both got into the car and started off for their sightseeing. John is very happy that he asked Dheeraj for this trip. He now feels that he has lived a typical Indian life for a day. But he is also aware that there are so many things he is yet to understand.

As the car got onto the dusty road leading out of the village, John saw a few men at a distance going into the fields with water tumblers/bottles in their hands. Now he understood their purpose. He also noticed women at a distance far away from the men.

"Dheeraj, why don't you guys build community Toilets?" asked John. "I understand the villagers do not have the mindset to have a toilet in their house. But as a community you can provide common toilets," said John wondering what the problem is.

"That is a good idea, John. In a developing country like ours, the priorities are sometimes skewed. Having public toilets is a good idea. But maintaining them is again a big issue. It is improving now. Even in the city many of the old shopping complexes do not have toilets, and even if they have they are not usable. The new shopping malls have world-class toilets now," explained Dheeraj and continued. "Hope the Government takes up and maintains public toilets on a war-footing."

"What is with all these animals on the road? I have not seen so many cattle yesterday," asked John as their car waded through the herd slowly, sometimes brushing against the animals.

"Sir, today - weekly market day," answered driver.

"Every week all the neighboring villagers assemble here with their cattle and produce," started explaining Dheeraj. "They meet here and sell their stuff. This is the place to buy and sell cattle as well as any other produce. People come out on this day to have fun also. Temporary arrangements will be made for having fun," said Dheeraj and pointed out to a carousel being set up for very small kids.

John had to look back, as the car got onto the main road.

"Dheeraj, I want to know about something I noticed in the courtyard of your cousin's house," said John leaning back in his seat.

"Go ahead, John," encouraged Dheeraj. John told him about the lady offering prayers to a plant in the courtyard, the ground wet with some weird stuff and the drawings on the ground.

"That plant is '*Tulasi*'," said Dheeraj. "It is also called Holy Basil. Hindus consider this plant as a manifestation of Goddess *Tulasi*. And we are told to protect the plant and pray to it every day to get a good life here and later salvation - *Moksha*. It is the responsibility of the women to ensure that the plant is cared for and watered every day. As usual, there is a big story about *Tulasi*, which I am not well aware of."

"Oh! I see. I will look it up on the internet. I am sure it would be an interesting one. But there should be some real practical purpose for it, what is it?" asked John.

"I like that question, John," said Dheeraj and patted John affectionately. "You are now thinking like a pro and trying to go beneath the surface to understand the practice. What do you decipher from the act of caring for the plant?" enquired Dheeraj.

"One thing is very clear. Whatever the story is, the rituals performed will ensure that the plant is kept alive. As I think more, it appears your elders wanted this plant to be protected," theorized John in Sherlock-Holmes style.

"Awesome! John!" said Dheeraj. "This plant has lots of medicinal values. Chewing its leaves gets rid of many ailments. It is called '*Sarva-Roga-Nivarini*'- a cure for all ailments. If you want every family to have this plant in their homes, what better way than to weave a religious story around it and make it a compulsory ritual!" said Dheeraj.

"I agree," said John.

"Have you heard about Swami Vivekananda - The Hindu monk who is associated with Ramakrishna Mission?" asked Dheeraj.

"No," replied John.

"He is well known in America too. He is seen in photos in saffron robes with a turban – the long cloth headgear. He was a Hindu monk, social reformer, philosopher and great thinker. Long back in 1893, he visited America and represented India & Hinduism at the Parliament of Religions held in Chicago. He is very well known for the speech he gave at that meeting. He got instantaneous applause and attention when he addressed the members as 'Sisters and brothers of America'."

"I can understand that now," said John. "You guys greet everyone as a family member."

Dheeraj continued, "He spread the knowledge of Indian spirituality, the *Vedanta* and *Raja Yoga* in West. He was a very rational person who despised superstitious beliefs and rituals. He wanted every human being to live the life to the fullest without fear and with a rational attitude. To communicate his ideas, to educate the masses, to transform people he chose the religious approach. He believed that only religious approach can influence mankind effectively considering the maturity of people," explained Dheeraj.

"So, what you are referring is that a rationalist, social reformer also adopted the religious way to communicate his message," summarized John.

"That is the point. As a teacher you need to choose an appropriate method based on the audience to communicate your message," concluded Dheeraj.

"As you are interested in Indian Culture, I suggest you read his books. He presents the ancient wisdom of India i.e. *Vedas*, *Upanishads*, *Raja Yoga* in a very logical & rational manner," suggested Dheeraj.

"I get it," said John and continued. "You digressed a little from our discussion."

"OK, OK! Let me explain the other stuff you saw in the courtyard," assured Dheeraj. "The weird stuff you saw on the wet floor – don't feel yucky – is cow dung."

"What? Cow dung!" exclaimed John.

"Yes. It acts as a natural disinfectant. So, it is mixed in water and sprayed on the floors. It is also made into cakes and dried for use as fuel. By the way, you can buy them online in India," explained Dheeraj and continued. "I am not sure whether you have noticed or not, in the village, we had come across people going after the cows and collecting the dung."

"The yellow color paste on the feet of women is turmeric. It is a powerful antiseptic, and it heals skin inflammations, lesions, scrapes. As women work barefooted it protects them well."

"Is it the same powder you use in food?" asked John.

"Yes, that is true. It has lots of medicinal values. For that matter, the spices that we use in curries have great medicinal values. It is not just taste and flavor, but real health benefits are associated with these age-old practices."

"What about those drawings?" asked John.

"They are called '**Rangoli**' – '**Muggulu**' in Telugu. I am not sure what to make of it. You will agree with me that they are symmetrical, beautiful art forms and make you feel good. Apart from that - it is my personal inference - it allows the women of the house to do physical stretching in the morning and it is meditative in a way thus allowing their mind to relax. It appears to me somewhat related to sand *mandalas* of Tibetan Buddhist tradition. They painstakingly create the *mandala* and then dismantle it after it is done," said Dheeraj thoughtfully.

"That is a nice explanation," said John. "You are good at connecting things," complimented John.

"There is something special about the material they use in *Rangoli*," said Dheeraj. "It is called '**Suddha**' in Telugu - white natural dust full of Calcium. Maybe it has some real practical purpose in olden days. But now people use all sorts of colored materials to decorate *Rangolis*," said Dheeraj stretching his legs and relaxing.

Both leaned back in their seats and lost in thoughts.

They spent the day visiting nearby tourist spots. As usual, John demanded explanations from Dheeraj for everything he found interesting. Even though Dheeraj is not an authority on many of those subjects, he shared his point of view with examples. And John loved it.

At the end of the day, the car dropped them off at the Railway station for them to catch a train back to Hyderabad.

◆ ◆ ◆

"What happened, John? Have you lost your way?" enquired Ashley, noticing John taking a U-turn and driving back a few blocks.

John was so immersed in narrating his village visit to Ashley that he missed a turn he was supposed to take.

"Sorry about that Ashley," said John demurely. "We are not far off. I overran by a few blocks only," explained John coming out fully from the flash-back.

After a couple of turns, John said, "Here it is! Ashley," and pointed out an independent house.

"We are late by 25 minutes," commented Ashley looking at her watch.

John carefully drove-in and parked his vehicle in front of the garage door and both got down. John rang the calling-bell, but there was no response. He tried a couple of times and concluded that his parents are not at home. He moved to the security system and punched in the secret code to open the main door. They picked up their luggage from their vehicle and moved into the house. As they entered the drawing room, John's phone rang.

"Is that you, John?" the voice at the other end asked. It is John's Dad. The security system has sent an alert about the opening of the door to him. His parents were expecting him as John had already informed them about his visit

"Yes, Dad. I and Ashley just got in," replied John. They had chatted for a few minutes and John gave the phone to Ashley. Ashley exchanged greetings with them.

"John, take care of Ashley. We will be back soon," said his Mom and gave information about the food available at home.

John picked up some food from the kitchen for him and Ashley; both slumped into the couch in the drawing room. John switched on the TV and started watching the ongoing NBA game silently.

John turned and looked at Ashley. She is completely involved in the game and enjoying it. She is appearing a little different to John now. Since he took a decision to marry her, John is in a dilemma whether he has taken the right decision or not. Dheeraj came to his mind. While in India, for any dilemmas especially work-related, he used to discuss with Dheeraj. He decided to attend the planned meeting-over-a-drink with Mike & Dheeraj.

---***---

9. The Scriptures

(Happiness, Marriage, Karma, Nature as God, Cow-Worship, Scriptures/Treatises/Vedas/Bhagavad Gita, Mindfulness, Yoga/Meditation, Godmen)

"To your marriage!" said Mike & Dheeraj; and raised the toast to John.

"Thank you!" said John and clinked his wine glass against their glasses.

They are seated in their favorite restaurant for a drink on Mike's invitation. Mike wanted to have a discussion with Dheeraj about the online course on Happiness that he has completed recently. There were a couple of things that intrigued Mike, especially the video about an Indian rickshaw puller stirred his mind.

"Hey, John! Lucky for you that I invited you. As you've taken a major life decision you need all the advice and wisdom from both of us for your survival and happiness," said Mike pointing to himself and Dheeraj.

"Don't scare him, Mike. Marriage is not such a dangerous thing," said Dheeraj.

John chuckled and sipped his drink without saying a word. Both Mike and Dheeraj took a sip too and leaned forward to pick up the snacks from the table.

"Dheeraj, I liked the talk you have given about life events," said Mike as a precursor to the discussion. "Recently I have completed an online course on Happiness. There are few references to the Indian way of life. I think you can help me understand them better," said Mike and waited for Dheeraj's reaction.

"Sure Mike, I will do my best," said Dheeraj bowing his head and stretching out his hands.

"Let me start with the Indian rickshaw-puller – Manoj Singh," said Mike and leaned forward. "As part of the course, we were asked to watch a documentary movie titled 'Happy'. In that, they showed this guy Manoj Singh – a very poor guy who lives in a small hut with many family members. He is a daily wage earner. What the family eats on a day depends on how much he earns on that particular day. But the most intriguing part is that this guy was found to be very happy. And Manoj declares that he feels he was the richest person. How is it possible?" said Mike throwing his hands up into the air and leaning back on his chair.

"I noticed that with many poor people in India," commented John. "I always found them to be happy even though they were in torn clothes and working very hard throughout the day."

"It is true," said Dheeraj. "These poor people live one day at a time. You can say they are happy-go-lucky persons. They do not have plans and they do not have worries about the future. Many of them accept their situations as they are. In short, they believe in the Indian concept of *'Karma'*. They accept their situation as destined by God."

"That is interesting! I learned that *Karma* refers to re-birth based on the good or bad deeds you have done in the past life," said John sharing the knowledge he gained while in India.

"The word *Karma* is interpreted in many ways. What you explained is a popular one. Many an Indian believes in that concept. For generations, the elite Indians, for their own personal benefit, ensured that lower caste people and the poor people believe in that. The lower caste people are made to believe that they are born into a lower caste due to their past life activities. And they are made to feel inferior," explained Dheeraj and paused.

"But, coming back to happiness," continued Dheeraj. "This concept helps people to accept things as they are without question. So they won't worry about others living a better life and they won't compare themselves with others. They become stronger both physically and mentally. They are content with what they have."

"Contentment! I understand it now. That is the key to happiness," said Mike with excitement.

Just then a waitress who was passing-by bumped into Mike accidentally. The wine spilled on to the table and onto Mike's trousers. The waitress apologized profusely and cleaned the area to the best of her ability.

John, noticing that Mike is upset, said "Mike, this is your *Karma!* It was destined to happen, so it happened. It is up to you how you react."

"You are talking about fate, right? The fatalistic take on things-that-happen-around-us" said Dheeraj. "This is exactly the way poor and lower caste people think," continued Dheeraj. "They have been accepting their condition as fate and continue to remain in that for generations. They adapt themselves to the conditions rather than changing the environment. It is a major struggle for them to come out of that belief and make a real progress" said Dheeraj and paused to take a gulp of beer.

"Unfortunately, this mindset of *Karma* has led to a tendency to accept things as they are. Many Indians won't protest, don't assert. Western approach to life is different. For example, the 'skyways' in this city of Minneapolis is your response to the environmental challenge. To overcome the problem of yearlong snow, you have connected every building in this downtown through skyways. It is amazing" said Dheeraj.

"Yes, I agree. But," said Mike and continued. "But… the other innovations and actions in the name of development are causing immense damage to nature. For example, global warming is a result of the thinking to tame nature."

"There has to be a balance. In Indian culture, every living thing is treated as God, in short Nature is treated as God," said Dheeraj and leaned forward. "The best way to preserve nature is to instill a reverence for it. What do you say?"

"I agree," said Mike. "Not only reverence, but instilling fear also gets the desired behavior."

"True," acknowledged Dheeraj. "Every society to protect their culture instills both reverence and fear. In the case of India every tree, every animal for that matter even non-living things like rocks that are part of nature are respected. It ensures that people participate in saving and nurturing the nature."

"Yeah! I noticed that Indians pray to cows," said John. "These cows roam freely on the roads and people feed it and pray to it."

"You are correct John. The cow has a very significant place in Hindu culture. In my opinion, it is for economic reasons. As you know India is an agrarian country. Cow plays an important role in agriculture-based societies. It gives milk, it procreates and provides more bulls & cows for tilling, and its dung is used as fertilizer as well as firewood. So there are so many economic benefits. In Hindu scriptures, there is a sacred cow called '*Kamadhenu*' which grants all wishes and desires. It is known as mother-of-cows."

"Maybe you should pray to *Kamadhenu*," said Mike to John.

"Why me?" asked John in a puzzled tone.

"To wish for a happy married life," replied Mike.

"I guess I need everyone's good wishes," said John in a low voice. "I was very excited when I announced my decision to Ashley. And we met our parents and communicated our decision of getting married. But for some strange reason, I am nervous and not sure if everything is going to work out well," said John in worrisome tone.

"It is difficult to see the future," said Dheeraj. "There are no guarantees. The best you can do is to evaluate your decisions based on the information available at this point in time. In your case, you have already lived with Ashley for quite some time. So we can conclude you have enough data to make a decision," said Dheeraj then turned towards Mike and said,

"What do you say, Mike?"

"I agree. You will never have 100% information for any decision. You do your best and leave the rest to your fate," said Mike.

"There is a 2nd interpretation of *Karma* that will apply here. Your good intentions will lead to good results. It talks about cause and effect. So, John, you did your ground work and you have good intentions. I am sure everything will work out well," counseled Dheeraj.

"Thank you Dheeraj, I hope so," murmured John.

"By the way," said Dheeraj. "These principles are recorded in treatises called '*Upanishads*'. They date back to 7th century BC. They contain the core philosophy of Hinduism."

"Wow! They are so old," remarked Mike.

"Yes, there are other treatises which are much older than this. They date back to 3,000 BC. They are called '*Veda*'s. They are four in number '*Rig-Veda*', '*Sama-Veda*', '*Yajur-Veda*' and '*Atharva-Veda*'. They are composed in the form of poems and hymns in the **Sanskrit** language. The interesting part is that this knowledge has been passed on from person to person orally as there was no written form."

"Orally! That is incredible," remarked Mark.

"It always amazes me, how people in those times could think so much," said Dheeraj with awe.

"To make it easy to remember the knowledge is presented in hymns and poems. And they address most of the life's questions. In my view it is an attempt by great minds of ancient India to unravel the mystery of life and beyond. The guidance provided by them to humans on how to lead a life is appropriate even in this modern age. It is amazing and very difficult to fathom how the people in those times thought about all this. It is mind-blowing."

"Do you think they can guide John in his dilemma?" challenged Mike.

"Not just John's, everyone's dilemma," said Dheeraj emphatically. "There is a specific scripture called *'Bhagavad-Gita'*. This is in response to the dilemma of a king **Arjuna** in the epic war of *Mahabharata.* Arjuna was pitted against his own relatives and teachers in this war. He was torn between winning the war and killing his own relatives & teachers. **Krishna** - the God and charioteer of Arjuna - counsels him about his duty. That counseling is applicable to all of us in our duties in this life."

Both John and Mike leaned forward to listen to Dheeraj clearly. The noise level at the restaurant was making it difficult for them to hear.

"The specific message from the *'Bhagavad-Gita'* is that 'focus on the duty you have to perform and not on the results'," stressed Dheeraj. "It addresses questions about emotions, relationships, ambitions, and life. It gives practical ideas to lead a happy life. It encourages people to think and do good deeds. It prods people to be focused on the goals and not to be swayed by emotions."

Turning towards John, Dheeraj said, "The message to you is 'enjoy the journey of marriage and do not think about the results'. There will be ups and downs in life, be prepared to handle them."

"Awesome!" said Mike. "In these days, life has become very stressful. This scripture '*Gita*', I guess might help. After all, we all want to be happy. That is the reason I took the 'Happiness' course. One of the techniques they advocate is Mindfulness. I want to hear your take on this," said Mike.

"Did you notice how you leaned forward to listen to what I am saying?" asked Dheeraj.

Both John and Mike became conscious of how they are seated and how they are leaning forward.

"When you are focused on my words, did you notice what was going on around us?"

"No, for all practical purpose I was only hearing your words," said Mike. John also nodded affirmatively.

"That is mindfulness. You are completely involved in the act of listening to me. The *Bhagavad-Gita* and the *Vedas* have elaborated on this. They have suggested meditation as a technique to gain mindfulness. This is mentioned as part of *Yoga*" explained Dheeraj.

"Let me ask you a question," said Dheeraj turning towards Mike. "You are having wine now, right?"

"Yes," said Mike.

"I am a novice when it comes to drinks. I saw you do something of a ritual before sipping your wine. What is the best way to enjoy wine?" asked Dheeraj.

Mike looked at John and Dheeraj. He did not understand why Dheeraj is asking this but decided to play along. "First, you should use appropriate glass for the wine you take; this is to ensure that aroma is retained fully. Once you have the right glass and the wine is poured in, hold it with the stem - holding it by bowl warms the wine. Swirl the wine and smell it several times, take in the aroma and flavor. Then take small sips to taste the wine. Let the wine stay in your mouth and roll-over all your taste buds for a few seconds before you swallow," explained Mike, and to demonstrate took a sip of the wine.

"You get the best joy out of the wine when you watch the color, smell the flavor, savor the taste. Use all your senses to feel the magic of wine," concluded Mike with an air of authority.

"Wow! Great explanation," said Dheeraj and clapped his hands in appreciation. John joined too and stopped when he realized that others are watching them.

"That is mindful wine tasting!" said Dheeraj. "Mindfulness is allowing all your senses to focus on the act you perform in the present. Whether it is eating, drinking, playing, working or thinking; just focus all your senses on that. That is exactly the Yoga & Meditation helps you with. These are documented in the '*Veda*'s."

"Yoga helps body, mind, and spirit," continued Dheeraj. "Apart from physical exercises/postures called '*Asanas*', Yoga includes breathing exercises and mind-control exercises also. This knowledge was kept secret for many years. And people were taught this under the oath of secrecy giving it a mystic aura. Recently one practitioner **Baba Ramdev** had made it accessible to masses and popularized it through regular TV programs and public demonstrations. Now every Indian irrespective of religion, caste, economic status can learn and practice Yoga."

"Yoga has been popular here in the USA too for quite some time," said Mike.

"That is true. The knowledge of Yoga is now spread all over the world. In recognition of that in 2014, the United Nations General Assembly declared June 21st as '**International Day of Yoga**'. By the way, this wisdom of Yoga has been attributed to one Guru, **Maharishi Patanjali** and he is known as the 'Father of Yoga'."

"I think you have lots of Gurus and Godmen in India, right?" asked John.

"Gurus, Yes; Godmen, a debatable idea," said Dheeraj thinking deeply. "In India, as I told you earlier, everything in nature is considered God. It includes humans also. Any person who does good deeds for society, they are considered as Gods. So, in our Telangana state, a mother & her daughter - '*Sammakka*' and '*Sarakka*' - who fought against the King's army and died, are considered as Gods. Unfortunately, these sentiments are exploited by wicked people to prop themselves as Godmen."

"Interesting, I heard in one of the states there is a temple for a motor-bike," said Mike.

"Yes, it is in Rajasthan. People do worship it," said Dheeraj and drank the remaining beer in his glass.

Mike lifted his wine glass sipped the last drops of wine from it. He waved at the waitress and asked for the food menu.

"John, hope you got some answers from the discussion we had so far," enquired Mike as he kept his glass on the table.

"Yep! I feel more comfortable with my decision now. And I am ready to face the challenges whatever they may be," replied John in a relaxed manner.

Mike picked up the menu card the waitress placed on the table.

Dheeraj leaned forward and picked another menu card and asked John, "So, what are the plans to celebrate your marriage decision."

John looked up from the menu and said, "We are planning to spend a few days in Florida."

---***---

10.Happiest Place

(Traffic Congestion, Karma, Queue System, Moksha/Salvation, Happiness, Rituals/Festivities)

John and Ashley got back into the motel after an exhausting day at the beach. Both are sun-tanned heavily and they are happy about it. John had a great time with Ashley at the beach. For that matter, he is thoroughly enjoying the company of Ashley. After his discussions with Mike and Dheeraj, his mind is now clear of all confusion and worries. He is feeling good about himself for having made up his mind to marry Ashley.

As they both lay down on the bed in their motel room, John realized that Florida never looked so beautiful earlier. He was here once with Ashley and few friends. Even though Florida is a known place for John, he is now feeling that everything here has changed for better and appeared very different.

He looked at Ashley. She has slumped into the bed with her face down on the pillow and her hand on his chest. Her face is red with the sun-burns and it appeared radiating for him. He noticed that she is very relaxed and peaceful. Just a few weeks back she was very apprehensive about John's parents' acceptance of their marriage. But the visit to John's parents' place had put everything to rest. She found them to be very caring and accepting. This trip to Florida was her idea to celebrate their decision. She loves the thrill of rides at Epcot Center and very fascinated about the Magic Kingdom.

◆◆◆

It has been half-an-hour since they joined the queue for the ride in Epcot Center. John noticed that Ashley is annoyed and restless. John decided to lighten up her.

"Ashley, we are almost there. I think we have to wait for another 25 minutes to get onto our ride," said John.

"Ok. I wish these 25 minutes pass by quickly," said Ashley with a tired look.

"I am sure it will if we do not focus on it," said John and continued. "Let me tell you something about time and India. In India, I have seen my team members commute for two hours to work every day, one way."

"Every day, that too one way?" exclaimed Ashley.

"Yes! That is four hours commute to work every day. Many of them are women, as women prefer public transportation to ride a two-wheeler."

"It must be very exhausting," said Ashley. "They should be paid for this time apart from the work they do."

"You are right," laughed John. "The challenges in a country like India are many. Even Dheeraj takes one hour to drive to his office due to traffic congestion."

"He must be cursing himself every day for this ordeal," said Ashley

"On the contrary, he says he enjoys that time," said John. "He uses that time for listening to his favorite music undisturbed. He says in spite of the heavy schedule and busy life, he gets two hours of personal time for listening to music and thinking."

"What!" exclaimed Ashley with disbelief.

"His philosophy is simple," continued John. "If you cannot change something, ACCEPT it; and see how you can make the best use of it."

"Is it related to the idea of '*Karma*' that you recently talked about?"

"Not really," said John and continued. "The "*Karma*" concept is used, sometimes, by lazy people & non-assertive people to justify their condition, to rationalize their behavior. As per Dheeraj, this misinterpretation is a great hurdle in the development of Indian society. People look at it as 'Fatalistic'. They can emancipate only when they realize that all are equal in the eyes of God and that they are equally capable of leading a good life."

John stopped and moved forward in the queue as the people behind him nudged him.

"For example, see this waiting line. Here everyone is treated equally. Everyone is given equal chance..."

"Not everyone," interrupted a person standing behind John. "See those guys who have '***FastPass***'. They have a separate line." Everyone around laughed at that comment.

"I agree," said John addressing him. "This system of First-Come-First-Serve which we take for granted is a great concept. It enforces equality. We respect it; and it is our culture."

"I just overheard you saying '*Karma*'," said the same guy and continued. "This is about re-birth, right?"

"I think Hindus believe in rebirth and reincarnations," said a lady who became curious about the discussion. "As far as I know the Hindus' goal of life is to come out of this cycle of rebirths and unite with the Almighty. If I am correct they call it '*Moksha*' or salvation/liberation."

"You are right," said John to her. "It is said that '*Nishkama Karma*' i.e. Karma without any expectations will lead to salvation. The way my mentor in India looks at '*Nishkama Karma*' is different. He says it helps you lead a HAPPY life here and now. No expectations; or fewer expectations help you appreciate whatever you realize."

"John!" shouted Ashley with excitement. "We are next," said she pointing to the ride's entrance. "We are here five minutes earlier than the waiting time they announced."

"See the practical application of the '*Nishkama Karma*' principle," said John to the people around.

Everyone laughed out loud realizing Disney World's technique of wait time display.

Ashley rushed to the ride as a kid and John followed her. It was a great ride. Both shouted like kids while on the ride. Within minutes they are out of the ride and started looking around for the next big ride.

During this ride also Ashley screamed, shouted in excitement. And she was visibly excited and looked very happy. John also enjoyed but did not feel the same excitement as he felt during his last visit. This is the 2nd trip for John and he realized that there aren't any new rides. He loves rides, he likes the excitement. But this time he is a little disappointed. There was not enough adrenaline flow. He looked around for MORE exciting, MORE Challenging rides; but could not find any.

Suddenly, he remembered his discussion with Dheeraj on Happiness. Dheeraj's words came to his mind, "John, when you want sensory stimulation from outside for your happiness or joy, your body tends to look for higher & higher doses of stimulation to get the same level of joy or happiness - a sort of 'law of diminishing returns'. Say, you want a certain brand of the car; you buy it and lose the excitement after a few days or months. To keep your excitement at the same level you now need a higher brand. And it goes on. It is the same case with anything in life. We need to realize that and *look inside* for happiness."

John believed in the proverb '**Variety is the spice of life**'.

But after his visit to India, his view of happiness has changed. There is a defined routine way of living that he noticed in India. The rituals that an Indian follows throughout a year keep them engaged with life. The festivals are spaced out throughout the year. Every 2 to 3 months there is an event to be celebrated. All religions have their own events. He witnessed the celebrations of few festivals such '**Ganesh Chaturthi**', '**Dussehra**', '**Holi**'. Every family whether it is poor or rich participates equally in these celebrations. Every year they look for these events; they repeat the same things again and again with the same level of excitement and joy.

"Come on John, let us join the line fast," said Ashley and dragged him to the line. It showed a wait time of 45 minutes.

"Let us hope this time we get our turn within 30 minutes," said Ashley remembering the experience at the previous ride.

"Don't expect any miracles, Ashley," said John to keep her expectations under control.

As they waited, they started discussing the next day plan of visiting the Magic Kingdom.

◆◆◆

At the Magic Kingdom also John had to catch up with Ashley's excitement. After the exhausting day, they went to the Cinderella's Castle to watch the grand finale of night-time fireworks show named '**Wishes**'. All visitors to the park assembled at that place. As Disney claims, John felt the Magic Kingdom as 'The happiest place on earth'. Both John and Ashley felt like spending every day of their life in this Magic land. It is so refreshing even though physically exhausting.

John identified a green lawn far away from the crowd. John & Ashley lay down on the grass looking at the sky for the fireworks to start. Ashley rested her head on John's chest as John held her affectionately.

"Ashley, did you notice that here in this park everyone forgets past as well as future, and they just live in the moment?" asked John.

"Yep! That is what makes us happy and that is the secret of this wonderland," said Ashley. She took a deep breath and lost in her thoughts. Ashley just realized that they could not discuss much about their future after marriage. They were just happy being together.

"John, can we go to India for our honeymoon?"

Before Ashley could complete the sentence, there was huge applause and the sky was filled with fireworks. Both joined the crowd in clapping and shouting with joy. As they lay down and watching the beautiful display of fireworks with Disney's iconic building the Cinderella Castle in the background, time appeared to have frozen. As they hugged each other, the fairy 'Tinker Bell' appeared above them in the sky amidst the background of the fireworks as if she is blessing them.

John felt himself to be on Cloud 9, and so is Ashley. Silently both thanked the Almighty for everything, and specifically for John's India visit.

As John thought about India and looking at the people around, he remembered Dheeraj's favorite saying in Sanskrit:

*'**Sarve Jana Sukhino Bhavantu**'*
– May all beings live happily –

⌘⌘⌘

Other books by the Author

Teamwork & Indian Culture
A Practical Guide for Working with Indians

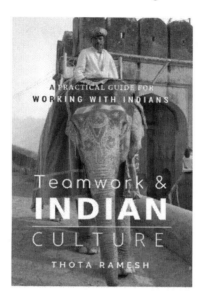

This is the first book written by Thota Ramesh. The success of this book prompted him to write "Daily Life in Indian Culture".

This book is about Indian Culture, focusing on workplace behavior. This book acts as a cross-cultural trainer for non-Indians. If you are visiting India for business, it prepares you well to enjoy your trip. This is a good companion book to India Travel Guide. **This Revised edition includes a chapter on "Chalta-hai" attitude of Indians.**

It explains the reasons for the typical aspects of Indian Culture, while focusing on the Teamwork culture in India. It provides guidance to people who want to interact with Indians effectively. This book analyzes the impact of Indian Culture on the work place behavior of Indians. It provides insight into how that particular behavior evolved, and also suggests techniques to overcome the negative influence of those behavior patterns.

Each chapter highlights one typical issue. It starts with John facing a problem then approaching Dheeraj for help. Dheeraj guides John in solving the problem. During this process Dheeraj shares some examples of his life and expresses his understanding of the reasons behind the situation, and gives suggestions on how it can be solved. This book addresses the common issues such as:

- Meeting deadlines at the last minute only, in spite of the team working for long hours
- The Yes Sir / Yes Madam culture
- The prevalent Communication problems with Indian teams
- The resistance to using the tools, sharing the knowledge
- The "Chalta-hai" attitude

This book is available at www.amazon.com

Being Happy is Easy
Go Beyond Positive Psychology,
Apply a Simple Technique for Eternal Happiness

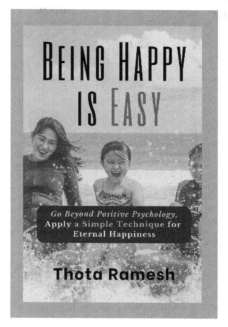

Live life the way YOU WANT!
And ENJOY it to the fullest!

Contrary to popular perception, *being happy is the ONLY thing that can be under your FULL control.* But the challenge is - to be happy even in the midst of a serious crisis such as COVID-19. The author did extensive study and introspection on how to live happily. He found answers in Spiritual teachings and in modern Psychology. He applied this learning and achieved being happy almost 100% of the time, at a young age. *With this approach you can raise your "happiness set-point" irrespective of the genes you carry. And you will learn to be happy in any situation.*

This book is a Practical Guide to handle work, relationships without stress; and gain eternal happiness.

- Do you get overwhelmed with many things that you need to take care of?
- Do you feel being exploited, ignored by your co-workers and sometimes by your family members?
- Do you find it unmanageable to control your anger, hatred, etc?
- If you are a parent, do you struggle to understand how to raise your children? What you should prepare them for and how?
- Do you worry about the future of yourself or of your children and other family members?
- Do you find it hard to ignore the past and struggle to focus on the present?
- Are you unable to enjoy the simple things of life even though you want to?
- Do you sometimes feel sad, depressed for not getting the attention that you deserve?
- Do you feel lonely and not understood?
- Do you wonder what life is all about?

**This book is a practical guide for
day-to-day happy living.**

Learn to be happy. *And Enjoy life!*

This book is available at www.amazon.com.

*** *

Acknowledgments

This book is a result of the encouragement I got from the reception of my earlier book "Teamwork & Indian Culture – A Practical Guide for Working with Indians". I convey my thanks to all those readers who bought that book; and my special thanks to the readers who had taken time to pen their reviews. The reviews have helped to promote the book and thus making it known to interested readers.

Once again, my brothers were there to review the chapters and provide instant feedback. I would like to thank, this time too, my brothers - T. Sudhakar, Lt. Col (Dr) T. Dayakar, T. Kishan Rao, Prof. Dr. T. Bhaskar Rao - for reviewing the chapters and providing feedback on the same.

I would also like to thank my wife Kiranmai, my daughter Sanjana and my son Pratyush for their patience and constant support.

---***---

About the Author

Thota Ramesh lives in Hyderabad, India with his wife and son (His daughter is married and lives in Whitesburg, KY, USA). He is currently working as a Software Delivery head. He is an accomplished speaker. His favorite topics include Behavioral Transformation, Emotional Intelligence, and Stress Management.

He is a postgraduate in Business Administration and in Applied Psychology. At a young age he learned Magic & Hypnotism to understand the working of the mind. He believes in educating people to see reason and to live happily. He strives to do his bit through seminars and writing articles/books. He feels the majority of human beings are good, but they allow bad things to happen as they are fearful and unassertive.

As a software professional, he had worked in many countries including the USA, UK, Zimbabwe, Egypt, Syria, Chile. His sports interests include Cricket, Table Tennis, and Snooker. And he loves playing Bridge with his brothers.

---***---

Manufactured by Amazon.ca
Bolton, ON